MATT AND TOM OLDFIELD

ULTIMATE
FOOTBALL HEROES

SON

FROM THE PLAYGROUND
TO THE PITCH

DINO

First published by Dino Books in 2021,
an imprint of Bonnier Books UK,
The Plaza, 535 King's Road, London SW10 0SZ
Owned by Bonnier Books,
Sveavägen 56, Stockholm, Sweden

@dinobooks
@footieheroesbks
www.heroesfootball.com
www.bonnierbooks.co.uk

Design by www.envydesign.co.uk

Paperback ISBN: 978 1 78946 471 9
E-book ISBN: 978 1 78946 470 2

British Library cataloguing-in-publication data:
A catalogue record for this book is available from the British Library.

Printed and bound in Great Britain by Clays Ltd, Elcograf S.p.A.

1 3 5 7 9 10 8 6 4 2

For Noah and Nico,
Southampton's future strikeforce.

Matt Oldfield is an accomplished writer and the editor-in-chief
of football review site Of Pitch & Page. Tom Oldfield is a
freelance sports writer and the author of biographies on
Cristiano Ronaldo, Arsène Wenger and Rafael Nadal.

Cover illustration by Dan Leydon.
To learn more about Dan visit danleydon.com
To purchase his artwork visit etsy.com/shop/footynews
Or just follow him on Twitter @danleydon

TABLE OF CONTENTS

ACKNOWLEDGEMENTS

First of all, I'd like to thank everyone at Bonnier Books UK for supporting me throughout and for running the ever-expanding UFH ship so smoothly. Writing stories for the next generation of football fans is both an honour and a pleasure. Thanks also to my agent, Nick Walters, for helping to keep my dream job going, year after year.

Next up, an extra big cheer for all the teachers, booksellers and librarians who have championed these books, and, of course, for the readers. The success of this series is truly down to you.

Okay, onto friends and family. I wouldn't be writing this series if it wasn't for my brother Tom. I owe him so much and I'm very grateful for his belief in me as an author. I'm also very grateful to the rest of my family, especially Mel, Noah, Nico, and of course Mum and Dad. To my parents, I owe my biggest passions: football and books. They're a real inspiration for everything I do.

Pang, Will, Mills, Doug, Naomi, John, Charlie, Sam, Katy, Ben, Karen, Ana (and anyone else I forgot) – thanks for all the love and laughs, but sorry, no I won't be getting 'a real job' anytime soon!

And finally, I couldn't have done any of this without Iona's encouragement and understanding. Much love to you.

CHAPTER 1

A SONSATIONAL
GOAL!

7 December 2019, Tottenham Hotspur Stadium

As Son Heung-min controlled the ball on the edge of
his own box, he could already hear his teammates
calling out to him. The counter-attack was on.

'Yes!' yelled Dele Alli, making a run to his left.

'Over here!' shouted Lucas Moura, unmarked in
the middle.

But while Son Heung-min paused for a moment,
thinking of the best pass to play, the Burnley defenders
backed away and a space opened up right in front of
him. So he kept going.

Why not? After all, Tottenham were already

winning 2–0, thanks to goals from Harry Kane and Lucas. Son Heung-min had set up the first for Harry, and now he wanted to score one of his own. He loved to dribble with the ball and a wondergoal would be the perfect way to impress his new manager, José Mourinho, especially after Spurs' disappointing defeat against Manchester United.

ZOOM! With a burst of speed, Son Heung-min carried the ball forward, leaving two Burnley players trailing behind. But now, he was dribbling straight towards two more defenders, and there was another one approaching from the right...

What next? Was it time to pass? No, Son Heung-min kept going. With two perfectly timed touches, he escaped past one player and then another. All of a sudden, to his great surprise, he was beyond the last Burnley defender and flying towards goal...

'Go on, Sonny!' the Tottenham supporters shouted as their excitement grew. 'Go on – what a goal this would be!'

Dele and Lucas were still racing forward in support, but Harry and Moussa Sissoko had both slowed down to watch Son Heung-min's spectacular solo run. They knew that their teammate had the speed and skill to go all the way and score, as he had done so many times in training. But to do it in a proper Premier League match was a different matter...

'Go on, Sonny!'

As he entered the penalty area, Son Heung-min slowed down to steady himself. And, he was starting to feel really tired after his seventy-yard sprint! But there was no way that he was going to rush his shot and waste this chance, not after running all the way from his own box. He was focused on finishing what he'd started. So, he waited for the Burnley keeper to dive and then coolly slotted the ball past him and into the back of the net. *3–0!*

Goooooooooooooooooooooaaaaaaaaaaaaaaaaallllllllllllllll lllllllllllll!!!!!!!!!!!!!!!!!!!!

As the Tottenham fans went wild all around him, Son Heung-min jogged over to the corner flag with his arms out wide and a big smile on his face. He felt so happy and so proud – what a magical moment! He had scored a lot of good goals in his career – for

Hamburg, Bayer Leverkusen, Tottenham and South
Korea – but never one quite like this. For a few
seconds, Son Heung-min just stood there, taking it
all in – the atmosphere, the achievement. Then he
nodded his head at the crowd; they had just witnessed
something truly special and chanted:

Nice one, Sonny, nice one Son,
Nice one, Sonny, let's have another one!

'Well done, Sonny, but why didn't you pass it to
me?!' Dele joked when he finally caught up with
his friend. Harry was the next to arrive and he too
hugged his teammate tightly. Lucas, meanwhile,
just clapped and clapped like the 58,000 fans in
the crowd. What else could you do after watching
a wondergoal like that!

At the final whistle, it was Tottenham 5 Burnley 0,
but there was only one goal that everyone was talking
about.

'Wow,' Gary Lineker tweeted. 'Son has just scored
one of the greatest individual goals you're ever likely
to see.'

And England legend Alan Shearer agreed. 'It will

be getting goal of the season, won't it?' he predicted on *Match of the Day*. 'They might as well shut the competition now.' He was right about that, and after winning the Premier League award, Son Heung-min's wondergoal would go on to win the 2020 FIFA Puskás Award, a prestigious award given for the best goal scored across the whole world!

However, when he spoke to the media just minutes after scoring that beauty against Burnley, Son Heung-min was as modest as ever. 'It was really important for us to get three points again,' he said, before thanking his Tottenham teammates, his manager, and the club's supporters. 'I'm just really grateful.'

Although Son Heung-min was an amazing attacker who could score great goals, it was his winning personality that made the Premier League fall in love with him – his humble attitude, his remarkable work-rate, all the smiles and all the handshakes. That's what made the South Korean such a special superstar, and as with so many things in his life, he had his father to thank for that.

CHAPTER 2

LIKE FATHER, LIKE SONS

'I just want to see if he likes it,' Son Woong-jung assured his wife, Eun Ja Kil, as he placed a small football at his son's tiny feet. At last, after months of waiting, the boy had learned to walk and so it was time for the big experiment to begin. 'If he doesn't like it, that's fine – we'll find him another passion. No problem at all!'

But secretly, Son Woong-jung had all his fingers and toes firmly crossed, hoping that his child would want to follow in his own footballing footsteps. As a young forward, he had played in South Korea's K League 1 and he had even been called up to the national B team, but sadly, an Achilles injury had ended his career early, at the age of only twenty-eight. And so, he had returned to his home city of Chuncheon in the north of the country to coach the game he loved and hopefully, raise a family of fantastic footballers...

Son Woong-jung held his breath as the boy studied the ball in front of him with curiosity. He looked a little suspicious of it at first, but eventually he pulled his little right leg back and *KICK!* He sent the ball rolling slowly across the living room floor.

'That's it – well done!' Son Woong-jung cheered with joy, before turning to his wife. 'See, he loves it already!'

The experiment was an instant success – Son Heung-yun was going to be a footballer just like his father, and so too was his younger brother, Son Heung-min, who was born three years later. Before long, both boys were dreaming of becoming famous professional players at the biggest clubs in England and making their family proud. They knew that it wouldn't be easy to go from Asia all the way to Europe, but at least they had their football-mad father to help guide them.

'Up you get,' he said every morning, waking them

extra early. 'It's time to practise!'

Whatever the weather, the three of them would
then head outside onto their local school's football
field, which Son Woong-jung helped to keep in
perfect condition. Every day, he cleared away any
litter and stones before they began to play, and in
winter, he poured salt over the pitch to make the
snow melt more quickly.

'Right, let's get started!'

Their father, however, wasn't a fan of the traditional
training methods used at all the football academies in
South Korea. He didn't believe in doing lots and lots
of running and fitness work at a young age; in fact,
he blamed that for his career-ending injury. So instead,
he came up with his own special plan for turning his
two sons into top professionals.

During their daily sessions, Son Heung-yun and Son
Heung-min didn't do any sprinting,

Or shooting,

Or 1 vs 1 battles,

Or play any matches against other kids.

That would all come later in their careers, according

to their father, and would happen once they were teenagers. For now, they needed to focus on mastering the basics: control, dribbling and passing. Son Woong-jung wanted his boys to feel comfortable on the ball. And to make sure their skills were as strong as they could be, they did the same drills over and over again. This became pretty boring by the twentieth time, but:

'Trust me, this is how you'll become the best,' Son Woong-jung told them. 'Once you've mastered the basics, there'll be no stopping you!'

Alongside the repetitive skills sessions, their father also taught them important life lessons. He wanted his sons to stay humble and respectful, no matter how successful they became. 'If your opponent gets injured, you should stop and help them, even if you're through on goal.'

'What, even if I'm about to score the winning goal?' Son Heung-min asked, looking a little confused.

'Yes, it's the right thing to do.'

'Okay, Appa.'

Throughout his childhood in Chuncheon, Son Heung-min never skipped a single training session.

He wanted to be a footballer more than anything in the world, and so he listened carefully to all of his father's advice, and he worked hard to put it into practice on the pitch. Son Woong-jung wasn't an easy man to impress, though, and he could be very strict if he didn't think his sons were taking his football sessions seriously.

'STOP!' he sometimes called out if he wasn't happy with their efforts. 'Not good enough, boys – what's got into you today? Stop squabbling and concentrate! If you want to be world-class players one day, then you need to show dedication and discipline, as well as passion. Right, I want you to do four hours of keepy-uppies – and if you let the ball drop, you have to start again. Okay?'

'Yes, Appa.'

Despite all the early mornings, the healthy dinners and his father's strange punishments, Son Heung-min remained determined to achieve his dream. It would all be worth it in the end if he could become a world-famous footballer.

CHAPTER 3

THE TAEGEUK WARRIORS OF 2002

Thanks to their father, 'The Beautiful Game' had always been big in the Son household, but in 2002, football fever swept across the whole nation. That's because South Korea were hosting the World Cup with Japan!

It was a massive moment for Asian football, but would either team do well in the tournament? South Korea had never got past the group stage before, while it was only Japan's second-ever World Cup appearance. The pressure was on – it would be very embarrassing if both host nations lost all their games and went out in the first round...

'No way, we're good enough to beat the USA and

Poland,' Son Heung-min told his brother with the total confidence of a ten-year-old, 'and maybe even Portugal too!'

Although that was a bold prediction, Asian football was certainly on the rise. More and more talented young players were emerging and making the big move to Europe. Japan had young midfielders Shinji Ono and Junichi Inamoto, who played for Feyenoord and Arsenal respectively, plus Parma's Hidetoshi Nakata, the most expensive Asian player ever.

And South Korea? Well, their strikers Seol Ki-hyeon and Ahn Jung-hwan starred for clubs in Belgium and Italy, but the rest of the squad still played at home in Asia for now, either in the K League or in Japan's J League. They had a great coach, called Guus Hiddink, who knew how to get the best out of his players and turn them into a winning team. After all, he had even managed the mighty Real Madrid!

That's why Son Heung-min was feeling so optimistic about his country's World Cup chances. 'Come on you Taegeuk Warriors!' he chanted at the TV screen as the South Korea team walked out onto the pitch in

Busan for their opening game against Poland. He was so jealous of the 45,000 lucky home fans who were there in the stadium watching.

'The atmosphere must be AMAZING!' he thought to himself.

But the Sons had created their own wall of red in their living room in Chuncheon, and they were making plenty of noise too. By the time the national anthems ended, and the players took up their positions for kick-off, Son Heung-min was buzzing with nervous excitement. And that excitement only grew as the match went on...

In the twenty-sixth minute, Lee Eul-yong crossed from the left and Hwang Sun-hong swept the ball into the bottom corner. *1–0!*

'Yesssssssss!'

And in the fifty-third minute, Yoo Sang-chul danced his way through the defence, before firing a long-range rocket past Jerzy Dudek. *2–0!*

'YESSSSSSSS!'

'I told you we'd beat Poland!' Son Heung-min smugly reminded his brother.

What a win and what a start for South Korea at the 2002 World Cup! Now, could they keep it going against USA? Late in the second half, the Taegeuk Warriors were losing 1–0, but they never gave up, not with nearly 60,000 fans cheering them on in the Daegu World Cup Stadium, as well as millions more watching at home on TV.

'Come on, you can do it!' Son Heung-min urged his team forward.

When South Korea won a free kick near the halfway line, up stepped Lee Chun-soo to curl a long ball into the USA box. And up jumped Ahn Jung-hwan to flick the ball into the far corner of the net. *1–1!*

'YESSSSSSSS!' Son Heung-min cried out with joy and relief.

A draw was a decent result, but it did mean that South Korea weren't through to the Round of 16 just yet. To get there, they would have to avoid defeat against a Portugal team featuring Luís Figo and Rui Costa. That wouldn't be easy, especially as they had just thrashed Poland 4–0.

The Taegeuk Warriors, however, were determined

to win the battle. They ran and ran, defending tirelessly all over the pitch. The longer the game stayed 0–0, the more frustrated the Portugal players grew. First, João Pinto was sent off for a reckless tackle and then in the second half, Beto received a second yellow card. It was now 11 vs 9 – surely this was South Korea's best chance to pull off a famous World Cup upset!

With twenty minutes to go, Lee Young-pyo hit a high cross from the left, which looped down towards Park Ji-sung at the back post. Everything seemed to be in slow motion:

Park Ji-sung chested the ball down,

Flicked it up over Sérgio Conceição,

And then smashed a shot through Vítor Baía's legs.

1–0 to South Korea!

For a second, Son Heung-min just sat there, stunned by what he had seen. Had that really happened? Wow, what a goal! Everything about it was excellent, including the celebration.

'Shhhhhhhhh!' Park gestured, putting a finger to his lips.

It was a magical moment that Son Heung-min would never, ever forget. He had a new number one football hero now: Park Ji-sung. After watching the second replay, he suddenly sprang into life again. He jumped up on the sofa to celebrate in style, and for once, his father didn't tell him off for doing it.

'Keep going! Hold on! What a save!'

Son Heung-min and his family cheered and cheered until at last the final whistle blew. They had done it; not only had the Taegeuk Warriors just beaten Portugal, but they had also qualified for the Round of 16 for the first time ever! It was a very proud night for the people of South Korea.

The next morning, however, it was time to move on and prepare for their next opponents: three-time World Champions, Italy. The Azzurri had Paolo Maldini in defence and an attack that featured Francesco Totti, Christian Vieri and Alessandro Del Piero! Everyone expected them to thrash South Korea, but the Taegeuk Warriors were enjoying their role as tournament hosts and underdogs. Despite conceding an early goal, they never gave up hope of another

World Cup miracle. And neither did their number one fan, Son Heung-min.

'Come on, all we need is one goal to take it to extra-time!' he muttered anxiously under his breath.

And at last, it arrived. With the final whistle fast approaching, Christian Panucci made a mess of his clearance and the ball dropped down kindly right in front of Seol Ki-hyeon. *BANG!... 1–1!*

'Yessssss, game on!' Son Heung-min cried out as he danced around his living room.

Then, just when it looked like the game was going to penalties, South Korea scored again. As another cross looped in, Ahn Jung-hwan outjumped Maldini in the middle and glanced the ball down into the bottom corner. *2–1!*

As he watched the ball fly past Gianluigi Buffon and over the goal line, Son Heung-min went absolutely wild. It seemed too good to be true – South Korea were seconds away from beating Italy, one of the favourites to win the World Cup!

And even after that triumph, the heroic Taegeuk Warriors weren't done yet. They beat Spain on penalties in the quarter-finals to set up a semi-final against Germany. South Korea were now just one win away from the World Cup Final! But sadly, it wasn't to be. The Taegeuk Warriors stayed strong for seventy-five minutes but eventually Germany scored to end their remarkable run.

Still, what a World Cup it had been for South Korea, beating Portugal, Italy and Spain on their way to the semi-finals. Park Ji-sung, Lee Young-pyo, Seol Ki-hyeon, Ahn Jung-hwan – they were all national heroes now. Not only had they brought pride and joy to their country, but they had also inspired the next generation. Sitting at home in Chuncheon, Son Heung-min couldn't wait to become a Taegeuk Warrior too.

CHAPTER 4

BATTLES BETWEEN BROTHERS

'If I could be any South Korea player, I'd be Ahn Jung-hwan,' Son Heung-yun argued as he sat playing video games with his younger brother after school. 'No-one will ever forget his goals at the 2002 World Cup – he'll be a national hero forever!'

Son Heung-min, of course, had a different answer. 'Yes, but that was three years ago now! What's he done since then? Nothing! Park Ji-sung scored that amazing goal against Portugal—'

'So what? Ahn scored more!'

'I know, but Park won two league titles with PSV Eindhoven and now he's just signed for Manchester United—'

'Yeah well, Ahn will be playing in Europe too this season, for Metz—'

'Did you hear me? MANCHESTER UNITED!' Son Heung-min repeated, and those two words were enough to win the debate. For now, anyway.

Despite their father's best attempts to keep them focused on their own individual skills, they couldn't help competing against each other in everything they did. They were brothers, after all! So, whether they were discussing their favourite football heroes or playing video games, they were both totally determined to win...

'Yessssss, what a goal!' Son Heung-min shouted suddenly, dropping his gaming controller to do a victory dance around the room. All of those hours spent secretly practising on his own had finally paid off because he had just beaten his older brother. 'Park Ji-sung scores the winner! Sorry, maybe next time, yeah?'

'Whatever, that was a definite foul on my defender – the referee's rubbish!'

And the battles between the brothers became even fiercer when Son Woong-jung finally decided that his sons were ready for the next step in his special coaching plan: shooting. At last! The exercise wasn't quite as simple as just firing the ball into the net, though.

'I want you to take the first shot with your right foot and then the second with your left,' Son Woong-jung explained. 'We'll keep practising until they're both as strong as each other!'

'You can go first,' Son Heung-yun said, making it seem like a kind, generous offer, but Son Heung-min knew his brother too well to believe that.

'Thanks, let me show you how it's done,' he replied with a confident look on his face.

And so, their latest battle began. Son Heung-min set to work on beating his brother (again!) and becoming a brilliant goalscorer with both feet.

Right foot, left foot,
Right foot, left foot...

'No, don't just blast the ball as hard as you can – aim for one of the corners and make your shot accurate!'

'You need to hit it harder with your left foot – a keeper would have saved that easily!'

As always, Son Heung-min listened carefully to

his father's instructions. He was a fast and willing learner with a fierce desire to improve. No matter what, he kept going and he kept smiling. After all, he was playing football, his favourite sport! Even when he missed a few shots and started to feel frustrated, he kept working hard on his game. There was lots more to do if he was going to become 'the next Park Ji-sung'! The bright lights of European football were waiting for him, and so he wanted to progress as quickly as possible. Before long, he was shooting with power and accuracy in both feet, and scoring goal after goal.

'Very good!' his father praised him. 'It's time to up your game, Son Heung-yun – he's showing you up here!'

It felt so humiliating to lose to someone three years younger, especially when it was his own brother. But the harder Son Heung-yun tried to score, the more shots he missed.

'Arghhhh!' he snarled after firing another wild strike wide.

'Come on, concentrate! Listen to what I'm telling

you – pick your spot and aim.'

Unlike his brother, however, Son Heung-yun wasn't very good at staying calm and receiving feedback from his father. When things weren't going well, he really didn't like being told what to do.

'Just leave me alone!' he shouted angrily as he stormed off the pitch.

But Son Heung-min wasn't going to let his brother's temper stop his training sessions. Yes, he had already won their shooting battle, but he was aiming for bigger and better things. With each goal he scored, he got a little bit closer to his dream of one day playing competitive football, first in South Korea and then in Europe. But for now, he was happy to keep up the hard work at home:

Right foot, left foot,
Right foot, left foot...

CHAPTER 5

STARTING OUT AT FC SEOUL

When Son Heung-min finally started playing competitive football at the age of fourteen, he felt very grateful for his father's special kind of coaching. All those repetitive drills had really helped him to stand out from the rest as an amazing attacker. There weren't many young players in South Korea who could pass and dribble the ball so skilfully, or who could shoot so accurately with both feet.

GOAL!

And despite not doing much fitness work with his father, Son Heung-min could still sprint past any defender he faced. He had a brilliant burst of speed as well as a strong desire to win.

GOAL!

'Wow, what a talent!' his youth coaches marvelled, 'That kid will go far!'

For now, though, Son Heung-min was just enjoying every minute of his first taste of competitive football. He raced around the pitch with a beaming smile on his face, not wanting the matches to ever end. At last, his long wait was over! He was battling against the best young defenders in the city and beating them. And most importantly of all, he was part of a team now. Whenever he scored a great goal or they won a game, the players celebrated together with hugs and high-fives.

'Sonny, you're unstoppable! What would we do without you?'

Two years and many magical performances later, Son Heung-min was ready to take his next big step by signing for one of the top teams in the country.

FC Seoul had won the K League title three times and their academy had helped produce many of South Korea's best-ever players, including three of the Taegeuk Warriors of 2002: Choi Yong-soo, Choi

Tae-uk, and the team's star left back, Lee Young-pyo.

'It was his cross that set up Park Ji-sung for his wondergoal against Portugal!' Son Heung-min remembered excitedly, replaying the moment in his head.

It was a great honour to be joining the same club as a national hero like Lee Young-pyo. After the World Cup, the left back had signed for PSV Eindhoven and then two years later, he was playing for Tottenham Hotspur in the Premier League!

And Lee Young-pyo was far from the only FC Seoul player who had set off on an exciting European adventure. When Son Heung-min arrived in 2008, the team's star striker Park Chu-young had just moved to French club Monaco. Then soon afterwards, their midfielder Ki Sung-yueng signed for the Scottish side Celtic, while winger Lee Chung-yong went to Bolton Wanderers.

'That could be me one day!' Son Heung-min allowed himself to dream.

But for now, he was focused on progressing through the ranks at FC Seoul – from the Under-18s to the

Reserves, and then to the First Team. That was his plan, and he was determined to achieve it as quickly as possible. Ki Sung-yueng had made his senior debut in the K League when he was only eighteen, so why couldn't Son Heung-min do the same? In fact, why couldn't he go even further and become FC Seoul's next superstar at the age of seventeen instead?

'Anything is possible if I work hard enough,' he told himself with his usual positivity.

Son Heung-min treated every single moment at FC Seoul as an opportunity to learn. When the club invited him to be a ball boy at their home games, he jumped at the chance. Why? Because it was a great way for him to study the club's senior professionals up close. Sitting beside the pitch at the Seoul World Cup Stadium, he could hear everything the players said to each other, watch the clever runs the attackers made, and admire all their silky skills.

'Cool, I'm going to try that trick at training tomorrow!' Son Heung-min said to himself, memorising the movements so that he could recreate them later.

He didn't mind if he got things wrong and looked a little bit silly in front of his Under-18 teammates. Why would he worry about that? Everyone made mistakes and they were all friends anyway! If he failed the first time, Son Heung-min would just keep working on the skill until eventually he succeeded, just like his father had always taught him.

'And once I've mastered it in training, then it'll be time to try it out in matches!'

CHAPTER 6

A EUROPEAN EDUCATION

As Son Heung-min finally began to settle into his new life at FC Seoul, Europe suddenly came calling, and a lot sooner than he had anticipated.

After their team's successful performance at the 2002 World Cup, the South Korea FA had decided to set up a new youth project, where they sent their best sixteen-year-old footballers abroad to train at famous academies around the world for one season. They believed that the experience of top coaching would help create an even better generation of Taegeuk Warriors for the future. A few players went to Palmeiras in Brazil, but most went to... Europe!

SC Braga in Portugal,

Then Reading and Watford in England...

'Pick me! Pick me!' Son Heung-min hoped eagerly as he counted down the days until his sixteenth birthday. It was his dream to play in one of Europe's top divisions and preferably, the English Premier League. His ultimate goal was to follow in the footsteps of his childhood heroes Park Ji-Sung, Lee Young-pyo and Lee Chung-yong. Son Heung-min watched every English match he could find on TV and he was so determined to play there that he had even started to learn the language. His family didn't have enough money to send him to Europe, but if he could just get a place on the youth project, it would be an amazing chance to make his dream come true...

When the scouts came from Germany to watch him play, Son Heung-min did his best to impress them with his skills. He was happy with his performance, but would he be successful? In August 2008, the South Korean FA announced their latest list of six lucky young footballers:

Kim Min-hyeok, Kim Jong-pil, Kim Hak-chan, Kim Dae-kwang, Lee Kang-in...

And Son Heung-min!!!

'Yes, I made it!' he yelled out with pride and joy when he saw his name on the list. 'Europe, here I come!'

But which club was he going to? Son Heung-min would be saying goodbye to FC Seoul and hello to...

Hamburg!

Although Son Heung-min was a little disappointed that he wasn't on his way to the Premier League, he knew that the Bundesliga was still one of the best leagues in the world. And Hamburg were one of the biggest clubs, just behind Bayern Munich, Werder Bremen, and Schalke 04. Their star players – Rafael van der Vaart, Ivica Olić, Paolo Guerrero – were all famous names to Son Heung-min. However, he knew nothing about Germany – the country, the culture, or the language. Oh well, he would just have to learn as quickly as he could once he got there.

'Work hard and make the most of this opportunity,' his father told him at the airport. 'I know it's only meant to be one year, but if you perform well, who knows? Maybe they won't let you leave!'

As he left South Korea behind to set out on his

41

exciting European adventure, sixteen-year-old Son Heung-min felt a mix of excitement and fear. Yes, his childhood dream was about to come true, but for the first time in his life, he would be living away from his family, without his father there to guide him, either on or off the football pitch.

Although there were two other young South Koreans training with him at Hamburg, Son Heung-min still felt a long way from home. Life in Germany was so different, and it took him a long time to adapt. For the first few months, he missed everything badly – the TV, the music, the food, and of course, his friends and family.

'I can't wait to come back home!' Son Heung-min told his mother tearfully on the phone.

However, while times were hard at Hamburg, when it came to playing football, he never let his focus slip. Son Heung-min was determined to do what he had set out to do: impress his coaches and earn a proper contract at the club.

The young man's footballing strengths were clear to see straight away: the speed, the skill, the strength, and the brilliant shooting ability with both feet. But what impressed Markus von Ahlen, the more he watched Son Heung-min in action, was the boy's attitude. Although a natural goalscorer, Son Heung-min was also a real team player, who never stopped running. He was an absolute pleasure to coach – he was polite and always wanting to learn and improve.

'I think we should keep him,' von Ahlen argued with the other Hamburg coaches. 'He's got everything you need to succeed.'

Son Heung-min did everything he could to stay in Germany, scoring nine goals in fifteen games for the club's Under-17s. As the season went on, his form got better and better, ending with a match-winning performance against Werder Bremen.

'No way, we can't let Sonny leave!' his teammates pleaded.

But when his year of European education came to an end, Hamburg still hadn't offered him a contract, and so he had no choice but to return to South Korea and FC Seoul.

Son Heung-min didn't give up hope, though; no, he

stayed as positive as ever. He had learned a lot from his experiences in Germany, and he was sure that another opportunity would arrive soon. After all, he was now an even better player, and he couldn't wait to show it at the upcoming Under-17 World Cup.

CHAPTER 7

SOUTH KOREA'S NEXT SUPERSTAR

South Korea's journey to the 2009 Under-17 World Cup had started a whole year earlier at the 2008 Asian Football Confederation U-16 Championship. Although they knew that the top four teams would qualify for the World Cup in Nigeria, Son Heung-min and his teammates weren't just aiming for a semi-final spot; no, they were there to win the whole tournament.

The young Taegeuk Warriors showed their strength by sweeping through the group stage in style, thrashing India 5–2 and then Indonesia 9–0. The new generation looked even better than the last!

'Come on, we're going all the way!' Son Heung-min shouted as he celebrated his second strike with hat-trick hero, Lee Jong-ho.

By the quarter-finals, Son Heung-min had dropped down to the bench, but he came on and scored as South Korea beat the hosts, Uzbekistan, 3–0. Hurray, they had secured their place at the Under-17 World Cup already! And next up, in the semi-finals, they faced their big rivals, Japan.

Sadly, Son Heung-min's super sub performance wasn't enough to earn him a starting spot, but he did get some game-time in the second half as he helped South Korea hold on for a 2–1 win.

'Yes, we did it!' he cheered at the final whistle, hugging Lee Jong-ho. 'We're in the final!'

In the end, however, it was Iran who were crowned Champions of Asia, not South Korea, after a 2–1 victory. For Son Heung-min and his teammates, it was a very disappointing way to finish the tournament.

'I know it hurts, but you should all be proud of your performance,' their coach, Lee Kwang-jong told them. 'Let's learn from this defeat and come back even stronger at the World Cup!'

Those words were still fresh in Son Heung-min's

mind as he and his South Korea teammates set off for Nigeria in October 2009. He was certainly ready to come back stronger. Thanks to his European education at Hamburg, he had become an even better player. So, this time, he wasn't going to be South Korea's super sub; no, he was going to be their superSTAR. The Under-17 World Cup was the perfect place for him to make a name for himself, just as top players like Cesc Fàbregas and Toni Kroos had done in the past.

'Let's go!' Son Heung-min called out to Lee Jong-ho as they kicked off against Uruguay.

Nam Seung-woo raced through to give South Korea an early lead, which lasted until the sixtieth minute, when Sebastián Gallegos scored an equaliser from the penalty spot. 1–1 – with two more group games to play, a draw wouldn't be a disastrous result for South Korea, but their new superstar decided they could do better than that...

As the free kick floated into the box, the Uruguayan defender panicked and sliced his clearance straight to Son Heung-min. What a chance! He had to make the most of it. His first touch was perfect, just like his father had taught him. And his second? A cool right-foot finish past the keeper. *2–1!*

Gooooooooooooooooooooaaaaaaaaaaaaaaaaalllllllllllllll lllllllllllll!!!!!!!!!!!!!!!!!!!!

Yes, Son Heung-min had saved the day for South Korea! As he turned away in triumph, he recreated Park Ji-sung's celebration against Portugal at the 2002 World Cup.

'Shhhhhhhhh!' Son Heung-min gestured, putting a finger to his lips. It felt so good to be following in his hero's footsteps.

With that win against Uruguay, South Korea were off to a wonderful start. It meant that despite a 2–1 defeat to Italy, they could still make it through to the Round of 16 if they beat Algeria. It was a must-win match for the young Taegeuk Warriors, but Son Heung-min wasn't going to let the pressure get to him. Instead, he stayed as calm and positive as ever.

'Come on, we can win this!' he told his teammates.

And they did. Lee Jung-ho scored the first goal and who scored the second? Son Heung-min, South Korea's next superstar! Controlling a long ball beautifully, he used his speed and skill to cut in off the left wing, before unleashing an unstoppable shot into the bottom corner. *2–0!*

Goooooooooooooooooooaaaaaaaaaaaaaaaaalllllllllllllll llllllllllllll!!!!!!!!!!!!!!!!!!!!!

Son Heung-min jumped up and punched the air, but not with his usual joy and passion. He was saving his best smiles until the final whistle...

'Yes, we did it!' he cried out, hugging each and every one of his teammates and coaches. What an amazing achievement! South Korea were through to the second round of the Under-17 World Cup for the first time in over twenty years, and they didn't stop there. They showed their strong team spirit by beating Mexico on penalties to set up a quarter-final against the tournament hosts.

With one more surprise win, South Korea would reach the World Cup semi-finals! Yes, Nigeria had the home crowd behind them and some brilliant young talents, but they weren't unbeatable. The Taegeuk Warriors just had to keep working hard and continue believing in themselves.

When Nigeria scored first, the South Korea players didn't let their heads drop. Instead, they fought their way back into the game, thanks to another goal from Son Heung-min, and this one was extra special. He was nearer to the halfway line than the penalty area when he got the ball, but using his strength and speed, he managed to escape from his marker and burst forward on the attack. Just as another defender rushed in to close him down, Son Heung-min decided to shoot. *BANG!* He sent the ball sailing over the keeper's upstretched arms and into the roof of the net.

Gooooooooooooooooooooooaaaaaaaaaaaaaaaaalllllllllllllllll llllllllllllll!!!!!!!!!!!!!!!!!!!!

What a sweet strike! Before he knew it, he was surrounded by teammates and coaches congratulating him.

'Yes, Sonny, you hero!'

'Get in, we're back in the game!'

Sadly, however, the match slipped away from South Korea in the second half. Nigeria scored twice to make it 3–1 and knock them out of the tournament. Still, the Taegeuk Warriors left the 2009 Under-17 World

Cup with their heads held high, and especially Son Heung-min. With three goals in five games, he had certainly achieved his aim. Scouts from all over the world would now remember his name.

CHAPTER 8

GERMANY AGAIN!

Although Hamburg had let Son Heung-min leave and return to South Korea, they hadn't forgotten about him. Their scouts kept an eye on his progress, thinking that one day, they might bring him back to Germany. But suddenly, after his star performances at the Under-17 World Cup, the club were forced to act fast.

'I told you we should have signed him when he was here!' von Ahlen reminded the other youth coaches. 'What are we waiting for? Let's get the deal done now, otherwise we'll lose him to one of the big clubs!'

Fortunately, Son Heung-min had happy memories of his time at Hamburg and he was ready to return and start his European adventure again. After he spoke to his father, the club were able to agree the terms of a contract, so that by the time Son Heung-min returned from the World Cup, he was officially a Hamburg player.

He was off to Germany again! It was exciting news for everyone, and von Ahlen was there to greet Son Heung-min as he arrived at the academy training ground.

'Welcome back! I was hoping I'd get the chance to work with you again.'

'Thanks Coach, me too!'

But really, Son Heung-min wasn't planning on sticking around for long in the Hamburg youth team. He was determined to progress as quickly as possible – to the reserves and then the first team. That was where he wanted to be, starring in the Bundesliga, and he knew that Hamburg had a good record of developing young players. Vincent Kompany, Rafael van der Vaart and Jérôme Boateng had all been at the club early in their careers – and look at them now! So, would Son Heung-min be the next to rise up through the ranks?

That was the aim, but first, he spent the rest of the 2009–10 season showing what he could do in the

Under-19s:

Two goals against CZ Jena,

One against Hansa Rostock,

One against RW Erfurt...

Son Heung-min was shooting his way to the top, one goal at a time. By April 2010, he was also getting game-time for the reserves, where he scored a worldie against Hertha Berlin.

'Wow, that was some strike, Sonny!' Rodolfo Cardoso, the manager, praised him. 'If you keep playing like this, it's only a matter of time before they call you up to the first team.'

Although Son Heung-min was pleased with his rapid progress, he didn't allow himself to relax. No, there was always more work he could do to improve as a footballer. That's what his father had always taught him.

'Hey, do you ever take a break?' his agent, Thies Bliemeister, joked. 'Every time I come here, you're outside training!'

During the few hours of each day when he wasn't practising his skills, Son Heung-min was doing his best to adapt to life in a different country. He met up with new friends in Hamburg and spent hours learning German by watching episodes of SpongeBob SquarePants!

'Hey, you're getting really good!' his teammate, Shkodran Mustafi, complimented him.

All that hard work both on and off the pitch paid off because by the time the next pre-season started, Son Heung-min was training with the Hamburg first team. Suddenly, he was sharing a pitch with top international players like Zé Roberto, Marcell Jansen, Mladen Petrić, Eljero Elia, and best of all, Ruud van Nistelrooy!

Yes, the former Manchester United legend was now playing up front for Hamburg, and at the end of Son Heung-min's first training session with the first team, the striker walked over to speak to him. Uh-oh, had he done something wrong?

'Hey, well played today,' Ruud said with a smile. 'Keep going, you've got a special talent!'

Son Heung-min was so shocked that for a moment he forgot his usual politeness, but eventually managed to blurt out the word 'Thanks!'. To get a compliment like that from such a world-class footballer was a big confidence boost. As he went to bed that night, Son Heung-min was still buzzing with the news.

'Ruud's right,' he told himself. 'I can do this – I'm good enough to play for the first team!'

And Son Heung-min got his chance to prove it straight away during Hamburg's pre-season friendlies. The manager, Armin Veh, gave him plenty of opportunities to impress, including against the Premier League champions, Chelsea.

The English giants took the lead in the first half through Frank Lampard, but their players grew tired as the game went on, allowing Hamburg back into the game. When Mladen pounced on a poor mistake from Yury Zhirkov to make it 1–1, the team pushed forward, looking for a winner. With ten minutes to go, Veh turned to his bench for a super sub: Son Heung-min.

'Good luck!' Ruud said, giving him a high-five as he came off.

'Right, what could I do to make an instant impact?'

wondered Son Heung-min. Tomás Rincón's through-ball was travelling straight towards the Chelsea captain John Terry, but Son Heung-min chased after it anyway. As he had learned from Ruud, a striker should always stay alert because you never know when something strange might happen…

As Terry stretched his leg out towards the ball, he slipped, kicking it straight to Son Heung-min. What a chance! In a flash, he was into the penalty area, with just Ricardo Carvalho to beat. The defender had plenty of experience, but Son Heung-min knew that he could outpace him every time. *ZOOM!* He sped away from Carvalho and fired a left-foot shot past the keeper. *2–1!*

Goooooooooooooooooooaaaaaaaaaaaaaaaaaalllllllllllllll llllllllllll!!!!!!!!!!!!!!!!!!!!

What a super-sub – Son Heung-min had only been on the pitch for five minutes and he had just scored the winner against Chelsea! Yes, it was only a friendly match, but it really felt like a big breakthrough for him. Son Heung-min was so overjoyed that he didn't know what to do next – run, jump, do the Park Ji-sung celebration? In the end, he just stood there, smiling widely, enjoying a match-winning moment that he would never forget.

'Yes, Sonny, what a strike!' Ruud congratulated him after the final whistle, and there was more praise to come from his manager.

'Son has real quality,' Veh told the media. 'At eighteen years of age, he can already do so much.'

Wow, he had clearly impressed his manager! And with Ruud around to give him lots of top striking tips, Son Heung-min was only going to get better and better.

CHAPTER 9

HAMBURG'S HOTTEST NEW TALENT

Just as Son Heung-min was preparing to make his big Bundesliga breakthrough, however, he picked up a bad injury. 'Nooo!' he groaned as he hobbled off the pitch. The timing was terrible – the new season was about to start! Now, someone else would take his place in the team, and what if they performed really well? His opportunity would be lost!

But despite his initial disappointment, Son Heung-min didn't let it get him down for long. No, not even a broken foot was going to stop him from achieving his goals. After missing Hamburg's first eight matches, he battled back to full fitness. Now, he just needed to wait for a first-team opportunity to arrive...

Ahead of their game against FC Köln, the Hamburg manager had some decisions to make, especially in attack. Who would he pick to replace Ruud, who was out with an injury? In the end, he settled for Mladen and Paolo Guerrero as his two central strikers, and...

'Sonny, you'll be on the right wing,' Veh announced.

Wow, amazing! A smile spread across Son Heung-min's face and his heart began beating ten times faster. He was about to make his Bundesliga debut, and not as a second-half substitute. No, he was starting, and if he impressed his manager, he might even get to play the full ninety minutes!

'Thanks for giving me a chance, Coach,' Son Heung-min replied respectfully. 'You won't regret it, I promise!'

What a match it turned out to be. After only fifteen minutes of football, the score was already 1–1. Both teams looked dangerous on the attack and dodgy at the back, but who would come out on top? Midway through the first half, Gojko Kacar got the ball in midfield and played a long pass over the Köln defence for Hamburg's new Number 40 to chase.

ZOOM! It was the opportunity Son Heung-min had been waiting for. He sprinted forward at top speed, leaving the centre-backs trailing far behind. The Köln keeper rushed out to the edge of his penalty area, but Son Heung-min was too quick and beat him to the ball.

'Go on!' he could hear the Hamburg supporters in the stadium urging him on.

What next? He couldn't let his team down by wasting such a great chance, but there was no time to stop and think. Son Heung-min just had to stay calm and score, like he had done again and again while practising on the training pitch with his father. With his right foot, he flicked the ball over the keeper's head and then with his left, he coolly passed it into the empty net, just as a defender tried to close him down. *2–1!*

Gooooooooooooooooooooaaaaaaaaaaaaaaaaalllllllllllllll llllllllllll!!!!!!!!!!!!!!!!!!!!

What a classy way to score your first goal! After watching the ball cross the line, Son Heung-min kept on running, past his cheering teammates and all the way to the Hamburg bench to give his manager a hug.

'That was for you, Coach – to say thank you for believing in me!'

As he ran back for the restart, Son Heung-min was bursting with pride and joy. Not only had he just scored a wondergoal on his senior debut, but at the age of eighteen, he had also become his club's youngest-ever Bundesliga goalscorer!

Even though his night ultimately ended in a 3–2 defeat, Son Heung-min still left the stadium with a smile on his face. It was hard not to feel happy when he was already on his way to becoming a Hamburg hero. Yes, his football future looked very bright indeed. A week later, he signed a new contract, keeping him at the club for an extra two years.

'Son Heung-min is the best prospect I've ever seen,' Veh even said.

The boy wonder didn't allow himself to get carried away though – this was only the beginning. Son Heung-min knew that he was still a raw talent, with lots of learning and hard work ahead of him before he could become a regular starter for the first team. So, during the rest of the season, sometimes he started and sometimes he was a substitute. But whenever he was on the pitch, his flashes of his brilliance provided excitement for the fans.

Olé! Son Heung-min used his skill to spin away from two defenders and dribble the ball forward.

Olé! With a brilliant back-heel, he burst away from his marker.

Olé! He tricked his way past one opponent and then another, weaving his way towards goal.

Olé! He poked a clever pass through to Mladen as he burst into the penalty area.

Olé! He struck a fierce low shot from the edge of the box, which unfortunately bounced back off the post.

'This kid is incredible!' the Hamburg supporters screamed.

As Jonathan Pitroipa raced up the right wing against Hannover, Son Heung-min sprinted through the middle with his arm in the air.

'Cross it!' he called out.

While the ball floated its way across the penalty area, Son Heung-min followed its progress carefully.

As it dropped, he jumped up and calmly headed the ball down into the bottom corner.

Gooooooooooooooooooooaaaaaaaaaaaaaaaalllllllllllllll lllllllllllll!!!!!!!!!!!!!!!!!!!!!!

After celebrating in front of the fans, he turned to show them the back of his shirt: 'SON'. Just in case anyone didn't yet know the name of Hamburg's hottest new talent!

CHAPTER 10

LEARNING FROM LEGENDS AND EXPERIENCE

In his quest to become a top footballer, Son Heung-min tried to learn as much as possible from the experienced players around him. At Hamburg, he had Ruud, who was always happy to help him. And in January 2011, Son Heung-min was called up to the South Korea squad for the Asian Cup, where he got to share a room with one of Ruud's old Manchester United teammates: Park Ji-sung!

At first, Son Heung-min was too shy to really speak to his hero. 'What on earth would I say?' he asked himself. 'No, I'll just make a fool of myself!' So instead, he studied the South Korea captain carefully. What did he eat? How much sleep did he get? What did he do to mentally prepare himself for the matches?

As Son Heung-min soon found out, Park Ji-sung was a model professional. Despite his tremendous talent, he still worked hard every day, finding ways to improve himself. It was so inspiring to see a legend leading by example.

As the youngest member of the squad, Son Heung-min didn't expect to play in many matches at the Asian Cup. Really, he was just there for the experience, and to learn from legends like Park Ji-sung. But in the final group game against India, the manager Cho Kwang-rae decided to bring Son Heung-min on at half-time. Why not? South Korea were already winning 3–1 and on their way to the quarter-finals.

'Good luck!' said Ki Sung-yueng, the player he was coming on to replace.

Son Heung-min smiled his biggest smile back. He was so proud to be one of the Taegeuk Warriors now. Although it felt like the game was already over, he did his best to liven things up in the second half. He ran and ran, until at last, a scoring chance arrived. When Koo Ja-Cheol played a clever, defence-splitting pass, Son Heung-min sprinted forward to reach it. The angle was tight, but he didn't even take a touch to control it; instead, he just blasted the ball straight past the keeper. *4–1!*

Goooooooooooooooooooooaaaaaaaaaaaaaaaallllllllllllll llllllllllll!!!!!!!!!!!!!!!!!!!

Son Heung-min made scoring look so easy. Making a heart shape with his hands, he stood there grinning up at the South Korea supporters.

Despite his goal, Son Heung-min found himself back on the bench for their quarter-final against Iran, and then their semi-final against Japan too. With the score stuck at 1–1 in the latter, Cho Kwang-rae brought him on, but at the end of extra-time, the teams were tied again at 2–2. Penalties! Sadly, South Korea's first three players all missed, meaning their tournament was over before Son Heung-min could even step up to take one.

'Hey, we'll bounce back even stronger after this,' Park Ji-sung reassured his young teammate. 'Remember, the World Cup is only three years away!'

But back at Hamburg, there was more bad news waiting for Son Heung-min. After only one year at the club, Ruud had decided to move on and join the Spanish club, Málaga.

'I'm going to miss you,' Son Heung-min admitted as they said their goodbyes. 'Thanks for everything!'

Without their star striker, Hamburg struggled during the 2011–12 season. After years of Top Four finishes, the club found themselves fighting relegation instead. Woah, what was going on? It was a very challenging situation, especially for an inexperienced youngster like Son Heung-min. Having started the season well, with super strikes against Hertha Berlin and FC Köln, the goals dried up completely for him. He didn't score at all in November, or December, January, or February… Where was Ruud when he needed his help?!

'Sorry, Sonny – I've got to try something different,' the new Hamburg manager, Thorsten Fink, told him, dropping him to the bench.

The delight of scoring on his debut now felt like a distant memory. But even during the darkest times, Son Heung-min still managed to stay positive. If he kept on learning and working hard, he was sure that eventually his big breakthrough would arrive. In the meantime, he would help his team in whatever way he could.

'Come on, Hamburg!' he cheered from the sidelines.

With four games to go, however, things didn't look good. Hoffenheim had just thrashed them 4–0, leaving them just two points above the relegation zone. And to make matters even worse, Mladen had picked up an injury, so Fink had no choice but to change things again.

'Sonny, you're starting today,' the manager announced in the dressing room ahead of their crucial match against Hannover.

This was it; his chance to be Hamburg's hero and help them stay in the Bundesliga!

From the moment the game kicked off, Son Heung-min raced around the pitch like a player on a mission. This time, he wasn't going to let his team down. He put the Hannover defenders under lots of pressure and waited impatiently for an opportunity to attack…

ZOOM! As the ball sailed over his head, Son Heung-min chased after it, reaching it just before it crossed the left touchline. Right, time to attack! With a stylish stepover, he burst past the Hannover captain and into the box at speed.

'Go on, go on!' the Hamburg supporters were up on their feet, urging him on.

Son Heung-min was running out of room, so with a clever bit of skill, he twisted his way inside and back onto his right foot again. BANG! Three defenders tried their best to block his shot, but it flew just past them and rolled perfectly into the bottom corner. *1–0!*

Goooooooooooooooooooooaaaaaaaaaaaaaaaaaalllllllllllllll lllllllllllll!!!!!!!!!!!!!!!!!!!!

As the crowd roared and the adrenaline rushed through his body, Son Heung-min was off, sprinting towards the subs bench with his celebrating teammates trailing behind.

'Sonny, what a wondergoal… hey, slow down and wait for us!'

When, at last, the final whistle blew eighty long minutes later, Hamburg had the win they so desperately needed, and it was all thanks to their young hero. Son Heung-min had done it; he had turned things around and saved the day!

'Yes, we're staying up!' he yelled with passion and pride.

Son Heung-min was already looking forward to next season. He was all set to become a Bundesliga superstar.

CHAPTER 11

BUNDESLIGA BREAKTHROUGH

The move started with Artjoms Rudņevs winning a header on the halfway line and flicking the ball on for Hamburg's returning hero, Rafael van der Vaart. All of a sudden, there were three attackers against just two Borussia Dortmund defenders…

'Yes!' Son Heung-min cried out as he sprinted through the middle.

On his way into the box, he weaved right and then left, before ending up exactly where he wanted to be – in between the two defenders just as Rafael delivered the cross. It was a striker's run that Ruud would have been proud of, and with a diving header, Son Heung-min sent the ball flying through the keeper's legs. *1–0!*

Goooooooooooooooooooooaaaaaaaaaaaaaaaaalllllllllllllll llllllllllllll!!!!!!!!!!!!!!!!!!!!!

Son Heung-min raced over to celebrate with Rafael, who lifted him high into the air. What a start – it was only the second minute of the match!

Early in the second half, Hamburg's exciting new attack was at it again. This time, Son Heung-min flicked the ball forward to Artjoms, who chested it down to Rafael, who threaded a perfect pass through to Ivo Ilicevic. *2–1!*

What terrific teamwork! The fab four celebrated together with a big group hug. 'Come on, we can score another!' Rafael declared with confidence.

He was right. For his sensational second goal, though, Son Heung-min didn't need any help from his fellow attackers. With speed and skill, he dribbled the ball all the way from his own half to the edge of the Dortmund penalty area, where he curled a shot into the bottom corner with his left foot. *3–1!*

Goooooooooooooooooooooaaaaaaaaaaaaaaaaalllllllllllllll llllllllllllll!!!!!!!!!!!!!!!!!!!!!

Wow, he had just scored an absolute wondergoal against one of the best teams in Germany! With a big smile on his face, Son Heung-min ran over to hug his happy manager.

'Yes Sonny, I knew you could be this good!' Thorsten Fink shouted emotionally in his ear. Like Veh, he had spotted Son Heung-min's smart movement and his huge potential. What a wise decision it had been to give the South Korean a starting spot for the new season.

That day against Dortmund, a new Bundesliga superstar was born. Son Heung-min didn't slow down and let his success sink in; no, he didn't want to end up back to the bench. It was time to kick on and prove that he was ready to become a regular starter. He wanted to play every minute of every match for Hamburg! So, through hard work and help from Rafael, Son Heung-min just got better and better.

Sometimes Fink played him on the left wing, sometimes on the right wing, and sometimes through the middle as a central striker. But whatever his position, Son Heung-min always worked hard for his team, and usually, he found a way to score.

GOAL! After another amazing solo run, he grabbed the winner against Greuther Fürth.

GOAL! He opened the scoring away at Augsburg with an awesome left-foot strike.

GOAL! He snuck in at the back post to help his team beat Mainz.

Suddenly, Son Heung-min was unstoppable and undroppable! What would Hamburg do without him? Thanks to their fantastic young forward, they were back in the top half of the table again and they even had a chance of qualifying for the Europa League next season.

'Come on, let's keep this up!' Fink urged his players and Son Heung-min was determined not to let his manager down. Plus, playing in Europe's top competitions had been his dream since he was a boy...

GOAL! He dribbled in off the left wing to score against Werder Bremen.

GOAL! Son Heung-min helped his team to destroy Dortmund once again. From 1–0 down, Hamburg fought back brilliantly to earn a famous victory...

Artjoms fired home from Dennis Aogo's cross. *1–1!*

Son Heung-min scored with an incredible, curling left-foot strike. *2–1!*

Rafael set up Artjoms for an easy header. *3–1!*

In the final seconds, Son Heung-min slid in unmarked at the back post. *4–1!*

It was his ninth Bundesliga strike of the season already and there were still thirteen games to go. Suddenly, his target of ten goals looked way too easy, so he switched it to fifteen instead. The most important thing, though, was helping his team to win.

'Come on, let's keep this up!' Son Heung-min shouted, echoing his manager's words.

Sadly, Hamburg's end to the season was very up and down. When they were good, they were really good:

Hamburg 1 Borussia Mönchengladbach 0,

Mainz 1 Hamburg 2,

Hoffenheim 1 Hamburg 4!

But when they were bad, they were really bad:

Hannover 5 Hamburg 1,

Schalke 4 Hamburg 1,

Bayern Munich 9 Hamburg 2!

Although they had other top attackers like Rafael and Artjoms, so much depended on their young superstar. When he was at his best, so were Hamburg.

Who scored both of their goals against Mainz? Son Heung-min!

And who got them off to a great start against Hoffenheim? Son Heung-min! He headed home the first goal and then unselfishly set up the second for Dennis.

'Thanks for the assist, Sonny!'

Unfortunately, after a disappointing 1–0 loss to Bayer Leverkusen on the last day, Hamburg finished in seventh place, missing out on a Europa League spot by just three points. Arggh, how frustrating to come so close!

But for Son Heung-min, there was good news amongst the bad. His Bundesliga breakthrough was complete, and with twelve goals, he finished tied with Artjoms as his team's top scorer. Plus, according to the latest transfer talk, it looked like Hamburg's hottest new talent would be playing European football next season after all...

CHAPTER 12

BAYER LEVERKUSEN'S RECORD BUY

At the end of the 2012–13 season, Bayern Munich had won the Bundesliga title for the twenty-secondth time, while finishing a whopping twenty-five points ahead of anyone else. For Borussia Dortmund and Bayer Leverkusen, it was the same old story. What could they do to compete with Germany's greatest and richest club?

The only answer was to make really smart signings. Dortmund had lost both their star striker Robert Lewandowski and their most promising playmaker Mario Götze to Bayern Munich. So that summer, their manager Jürgen Klopp replaced them with Pierre-Emerick Aubameyang and Henrikh Mkhitaryan. He also brought in a big, strong centre-back, Sokratis Papastathopoulos, to beef up the defence.

And Leverkusen? One of their top attackers, André Schürrle, was about to sign for Chelsea, so they also needed to find someone new. Someone who could play out wide on the wings, but also through the middle. Someone with speed and skill, who could also score lots of goals...

'Don't worry, I've got the perfect guy!' the club's sporting director Rudi Völler told the manager, Sami Hyypiä.

As he had shown against Dortmund, Son Heung-min was young, exciting, and explosive, and he had Bundesliga experience. In other words, he was exactly what Leverkusen were looking for! And best of all, he was affordable. When the deal was done, in the summer of 2013, they had paid less than half of the fee Chelsea had paid for Schürrle. What brilliant business!

'I can't wait to get started,' Son Heung-min told the media as he held up the club's red-and-black shirt and smiled for the cameras.

When choosing his next club, he had wanted to

stay in Germany and play for a team in the Champions League. And although Dortmund had also tried to sign him, Son Heung-min had picked Leverkusen, for two key reasons:

1) He believed that he would get more game-time there,

And

2) It was a club with a lot of history back home in his country.

In 1983, Cha Bum-kun had become the first South Korean footballer to ever play in the Bundesliga. And after starting at Eintracht Frankfurt, the striker had spent six successful years at Bayer Leverkusen, scoring fifty-two goals. So, for Son Heung-min, thirty years later, it would be a great honour to follow in Cha Bum-kun's footsteps.

He would also have a lot to live up to. Leverkusen were an ambitious club who wanted to challenge for all the top trophies: the German Cup, the Champions League, and of course, the Bundesliga title. And as the club's new record signing, there was a lot of pressure on Son Heung-min to start performing straight away...

On the opening day of the 2013–14 season, Ömer Toprak launched a long ball up the field for his super-fast forwards to chase. As Sidney Sam sprinted after it, Son Heung-min continued his run into the box just in case. Sidney looked like he was going to shoot himself, but instead, he set up his new strike partner for a simple tap-in on his debut.

Goooooooooooooooooooooaaaaaaaaaaaaaaaaalllllllllllll lllllllllll!!!!!!!!!!!!!!!!!!!!!

Pressure, what pressure? Son Heung-min was off the mark at Leverkusen already! After saying a big thank you to Sidney for the assist, he turned to the supporters and waved his arms up and down, as if to say, 'Come on, make some noise for me!'

There was lots more for the fans to cheer about when Hamburg arrived at the Bay Arena. As much as Son Heung-min loved and respected his old club, he was a professional, and so he approached the match as if it were any other, with the same strong desire to win.

With only sixteen minutes of the match played, Leverkusen were already winning 2–0 and Son Heung-min was on the hunt for his first-ever senior hat-trick.

'Yessss!' he yelled out as he sank to his knees after bursting between two defenders and then dribbling around the goalkeeper.

What a player, what a signing! Son Heung-min's former teammates just could not cope with his incredible speed and shooting. Hamburg bounced back to make it 2–2, but there was no stopping Bayer Leverkusen's record buy. When Stefan Kießling's blocked shot landed right at Son Heung-min's feet, he calmly curled the ball around the keeper and into the back of the net. *3–2!*

Gooooooooooooooooooooaaaaaaaaaaaaaaaaalllllllllllll lllllllllllll!!!!!!!!!!!!!!!!!!

'YESSSSSS!' Son Heung-min screamed, holding up three fingers to the fans. He was so happy to become Leverkusen's hat-trick hero!

And his crucial goals continued:

Two against Nuremberg,

And then another winner against Dortmund!

Away at the Westfalenstadion, Leverkusen pounced on a defensive mistake. With two quick touches, they moved the ball from Emre Can to Gonzalo Castro and then through to Son Heung-min...

ZOOM! The Dortmund defenders had no chance of catching him, but he still had the keeper to beat. No problem! Son Heung-min dribbled the ball around him and into the six-yard box. He had a tight angle to shoot from, but he made it look easy.

Goooooooooooooooooooooaaaaaaaaaaaaaaaaalllllllllllllll llllllllllll!!!!!!!!!!!!!!!!!!!!

'Come on!' Son Heung-min cheered, jumping up and punching the air.

Leverkusen moved above Dortmund and into second place in the Bundesliga. They were now only four points behind the leaders, Bayern Munich!

Sadly, Leverkusen's title challenge didn't last very long, but Son Heung-min made sure that they stayed in the Champions League places. He scored a wonderful goal against Borussia Mönchengladbach and then, on the last day of the season, he headed home the winner against Werder Bremen.

'Well done, Sonny – what a hero!' Bernd Leno, the Leverkusen goalkeeper called out, as he paraded his teammate around the pitch on his back like a king.

Son Heung-min's goal had saved the day, helping them to finish fourth, only one point ahead of Wolfsburg, and secure the last Champions League spot. Phew, what a relief and what a way to end the season!

Son Heung-min had good numbers for his first year at Leverkusen – twelve goals and seven assists – but he was determined to get better. As his father had taught him, there was always more he could do to learn and improve as a player.

The hard work would have to wait, however. The summer of 2014 was significant – because Heung-min was off to play in his first World Cup with his fellow Taegeuk Warriors!

CHAPTER 13

2014: A FIRST WORLD CUP TO FORGET

In the South Korea squad that travelled to the tournament in Brazil, there was no Park Ji-sung, or Lee Young-pyo, or Ahn Jung-hwan. No, the legends of 2002 had been replaced by younger players with lots of talent but less big tournament experience:

Sunderland central midfielder Ki Sung-yueng,

Mainz playmaker Koo Ja-cheol,

Bolton winger Lee Chung-yong,

Watford striker Park Chu-young...

...And, of course, Leverkusen star Son Heung-min!

Yes, he was fast becoming one of his nation's most famous and important players. It was his last-minute strike that had helped South Korea to beat Qatar and book their place at the tournament. So, could Son Heung-min go on and become a World Cup sensation?

That was the plan! He couldn't wait to play in the competition that had inspired him so much as a kid. His country was counting on him and he was determined not to let them down. South Korea had reached the Round of 16 in 2010, and that was the aim again four years later. First, however, they would have to get through a group featuring Russia, Algeria, and Belgium.

Beating Belgium would be very difficult; Son Heung-min had played against Kevin De Bruyne in the Bundesliga and he was only one of their many superstars: Vincent Kompany, Dries Mertens, Eden Hazard, Romelu Lukaku... But beating Russia and Algeria? That was certainly achievable, especially if the Taegeuk Warriors started well.

And they did. In their first match, South Korea took the lead against Russia, when Lee Keun-ho's long-range shot slipped through their keeper's gloves.

'Hurraaaaay!' Son Heung-min cried out as the players piled on top of their goalscorer.

Sadly, however, they couldn't hold on. Six minutes later, Russia equalised, and the match ended in a 1–1 draw. Oh well, it wasn't the opening win that South Korea had wanted, but at least they hadn't lost. And if they could beat Algeria, their aim of reaching the Round of 16 would still be alive.

'Come on, we can do this!' the manager Hong Myung-bo told his team.

But South Korea were in for a big shock. The Algeria attack tore through their defence again and again, and by half-time, they were winning 3–0. As Islam Slimani bundled his way into the box to set up his team's third goal, Son Heung-min couldn't believe what he was seeing.

'Why isn't someone stopping him?!'

What a disaster! South Korea were being outpaced, outmuscled, and totally outplayed. Was there anything Son Heung-min could do in the second half to help save the day?

When Ki Sung-yueng's long ball bounced kindly off his back, he made the most of that bit of luck. With a clever turn, Son Heung-min escaped from his marker and then fired a shot through the keeper's legs. *3–1!*

Gooooooooooooooooooooaaaaaaaaaaaaaaaallllllllllllll llllllllllll!!!!!!!!!!!!!!!!!!!!

Son Heung-min was delighted to score his first World Cup goal but there was no time for a proper celebration. After a quick punch of the air, he raced back for the restart because his team still needed two more goals.

Soon, however, that number went up to three, as Algeria's attackers passed their way through South Korea's dodgy defence once more. *4–1!*

'Noooo, we have to be better than that!' Son yelled out in frustration.

It was a devastating defeat, which left their World Cup dream in tatters. Now, unless South Korea could somehow beat Belgium, they would be knocked out of the tournament. They would be heading home in disgrace, without a single win.

'This could be our last chance to show what we can do.' Son Heung-min spoke passionately in the dressing room before kick-off. 'So let's put in a performance that we can be proud of!'

But although the Taegeuk Warriors battled bravely in their final group game, they couldn't change the end result: defeat. To make matters worse, they had been beaten by Belgium's B Team, who had also played the whole second half with only ten men. It was such a humiliating way to end a horrendous World Cup.

When the final whistle blew, Son Heung-min couldn't hold his tears back any longer. His South Korea teammates and coaches tried their best to comfort him, but it was no use – he just kept crying and crying. At the age of twenty-one, he still hated losing just as much as he had when he was ten and playing video games against his brother. The only difference was that now, the matches mattered so much more. The results didn't just affect him; they affected the whole nation.

'Sorry!' he wanted to say to each and every South Korean.

Son Heung-min could never stay sad for long, though. His anger and disappointment soon passed, and he was back to being his usual positive self. They hadn't performed as well as they had hoped to at the

2014 World Cup, but there was lots that they could learn from the experience, and the Algeria game especially. They needed to be quicker, cleverer, and more competitive in every position on the pitch.

'Right, let's get started!'

The South Korea players now had the next four years to work hard and prepare for the next tournament. Then in 2018, Son Heung-min and his fellow Taegeuk Warriors would come back stronger than ever to put things right and make their country proud again.

CHAPTER 14

EXCITING TIMES IN EUROPE

Back at Bayer Leverkusen, it was business as usual for Son Heung-min in the Bundesliga:

GOAL! He scored with his left foot against Werder Bremen.

GOAL! He scored with his right foot against Augsburg.

GOAL! GOAL! He scored one with each foot against Stuttgart.

After three full seasons in the German league, Son Heung-min now felt like an experienced pro. He knew all of the teams and all of their different tactics; all of the defenders and all of their different strengths and weaknesses. That wasn't the case in Europe, though.

There, everything was new and extra exciting.

'Bring it on!' Son Heung-min told his teammates.

Thanks to him, Leverkusen would be competing in the Champions League for the second season in a row. The previous year, they had been knocked out by PSG in the Round of 16, but the players were confident that they could do better this time, particularly Son Heung-min.

Despite featuring in all eight of his team's matches, he had somehow failed to score a single goal, and that wasn't like Son Heung-min at all. Yes, he had provided two assists, but he was supposed to be a great goalscorer! So, what was he going to do to improve his European record? The same thing that he had always done, ever since he was a young boy training with his father back in South Korea: work even harder and practise for even longer.

'Doesn't he get bored, doing the same thing over and over again on his own?' the Leverkusen manager, Roger Schmidt, wondered to himself, as he watched Son Heung-min taking shot after shot – right foot, then left foot, from every angle and every distance.

The team training session had ended hours ago, but the young forward clearly wasn't ready to go home yet. 'He's got a winning mentality, that's for sure!'

As the 2014–15 competition began, Son Heung-min was desperate to show what he was capable of in the Champions League, starting with getting Leverkusen through to the group stage.

As soon as he collected the pass from Hakan Çalhanoğlu, Son Heung-min was off, charging into the FC Copenhagen penalty area. He could hear Stefan Kießling calling out in the middle, but there was only one thought in his mind:

'This is the moment I've been preparing for: the moment when all my hard work pays off. It's my time to shine…'

Gooooooooooooooooooooaaaaaaaaaaaaaaaaalllllllllllllll llllllllllll!!!!!!!!!!!!!!!!!!

Son Heung-min stood there grinning widely as his teammates rushed over to congratulate him. At last, he was off the mark in the Champions League, and there was no stopping him now. In the second leg, he scored again, in only the second minute of the match.

Intercepting a defender's pass, Son Heung-min played a quick one-two with Stefan, before firing a shot into the bottom corner. *1–0!*

Goooooooooooooooooooooaaaaaaaaaaaaaaaaaalllllllllllllll llllllllllllll!!!!!!!!!!!!!!!!!!!!!

Son Heung-min slid towards the corner flag on his knees. That was more like it – the lethal finisher that the Leverkusen fans knew and loved!

With his confidence up, Son Heung-min couldn't wait for the group stage to begin. He was determined to keep adding to his goal tally, even against bigger and better teams.

As Karim Bellarabi looked up to cross the ball in from the right, he saw that Son Heung-min had snuck into the Benfica box, completely unmarked. *PING!* When the pass arrived, he didn't even take a touch to control it. He didn't need to. With a whip of his right foot, Son Heung-min sent the ball sailing straight into the top corner. *2–0!*

Goooooooooooooooooooooaaaaaaaaaaaaaaaaaalllllllllllllll llllllllllllll!!!!!!!!!!!!!!!!!!!!!

'Thanks, what a pass!' Son Heung-min shouted as

he ran over to celebrate with Karim. Suddenly, he couldn't stop scoring in Europe!

Away in Russia, Leverkusen were drawing 0–0 with Zenit St. Petersburg when they won a free kick in an attacking area. It was a long way out, but as they waited for the wall to move back, Son Heung-min and Hakan whispered excitedly to each other. They had a plan...

At the last second, Son Heung-min walked away from the ball, leaving Hakan to take it. But instead of going for goal, he played a clever pass through to Karim, who laid it back to... SON HEUNG-MIN! Now, he was definitely within shooting range. *BANG!*

Goooooooooooooooooooaaaaaaaaaaaaaaaaalllllllllllllll llllllllllll!!!!!!!!!!!!!!!!!!!!

What a smart set-piece! He rushed over to the bench with a big smile on his face. With a win in Russia, Leverkusen would go top of the group. Four minutes later, Son Heung-min scored again to secure the victory.

It all happened in a flash. One second he was standing still in the centre-circle, and the next Son

Heung-min was sprinting past the Zenit defence and sliding the ball past the keeper. *2–0!*

Goooooooooooooooooooaaaaaaaaaaaaaaaalllllllllllll llllllllllll!!!!!!!!!!!!!!!!!!!!

As he stood in front of the away fans, Son Heung-min jumped up and punched the air. Oh yes, he was really loving the Champions League now!

In the end, Leverkusen finished second in Group C, setting up a Round of 16 tie with Atlético Madrid. The Spanish club were flying high, with Diego Godín in defence, and Antoine Griezmann, Mario Mandžukić and Fernando Torres in attack. Wow, Son Heung-min and his teammates were really playing against the big boys now; could they prove that they belonged at Europe's highest level?

'Yes, we can!' they cried out with confidence.

Leverkusen won their home leg 1–0, but away in Madrid, everything seemed to go against them.

First, Son Heung-min's shot looked goal-bound, until Mandžukić just managed to clear it off the line.

'Noooo!' he groaned. So close!

Then, Mario Suárez made it 1–1 on aggregate,

with a shot that took a wicked deflection.

'Noooo!' Son Heung-min groaned again. What
bad luck!

In the second half, as Atlético pushed forward on
the attack, Leverkusen dropped deeper and deeper.
Although Son Heung-min was doing his best to create
a match-winning moment of magic, Schmidt decided
to replace him with a more defensive player.

What followed was the longest hour of Son Heung-
min's life, as he sat on the bench and watched the last
fifteen minutes,

Then thirty minutes of extra-time,

And finally, a penalty shoot-out.

'Nooooo!' he groaned again as Hakan stepped
up first for Leverkusen and missed. In that horrible
moment, Son Heung-min really wished that he
could be out there on the pitch, helping his team.
But sadly, his night was over and soon, so were his
exciting times in Europe. As Atlético jumped for joy,
Leverkusen dropped to the floor in despair. Penalties
definitely had to be the most painful way to lose a
football match.

Although it took Son Heung-min a few days to rediscover his positivity, eventually he saw the progress that he had made. Five goals in ten games – that was a clear improvement on his old Champions League record. And at the age of twenty-two, he was only going to get better.

CHAPTER 15

PLAYING IN THE PREMIER LEAGUE!

The Champions League highs, the hat-trick against Wolfsburg, the superstrike against Stuttgart – yes, 2014–15 had been another stand-out season for Son Heung-min. With each goal he scored, his reputation was growing; not just in Germany, but all over Europe, including… England!

Yes, as much as Son Heung-min loved Leverkusen, he still dreamed of one day playing for a top team in the Premier League, just like his hero, Park Ji-sung. And so, when one of those clubs tried to sign him, there was no way he could say no.

Under new manager Mauricio Pochettino, Tottenham were a team in progress, moving steadily up

the table. Their next target was a big one – breaking
into the Top Four, which would mean the chance
to play in the Champions League. However, to get
there, they were going to need more goals. Yes, they
had Harry Kane, one of the best strikers in the world,
but he needed support. The previous season, Roberto
Soldado, Emmanuel Adebayor and Erik Lamela had
only scored five league goals between them.

That was nowhere near enough, not if Tottenham
wanted to overtake their North London rivals, Arsenal.
So, who could they add to their attack? Their first
transfer target was Saido Berahino, but West Brom
were refusing to sell him for less than £25 million.

£25 million? That was far too much money to pay
for Berahino! The Tottenham manager had a much
better idea. He knew a fantastic young forward,
playing in Germany, who would hopefully be available
for a similar price...

Pochettino and his Head of Recruitment, Paul
Mitchell, had first tried to sign Son Heung-min a
few years earlier, when they worked together at
Southampton. With his speed, his tireless work-rate,

and his ability to shoot with both feet, the South Korean was perfect for the pressing style of football that the Argentinian wanted his teams to play. Sadly, on that occasion Son Heung-min had turned him down to join Leverkusen instead, but Pochettino still hadn't given up on signing him one day...

'Come on, what are we waiting for?' the manager told Mitchell and the Tottenham chairman, Daniel Levy. 'Go and get our man!'

When Son Heung-min heard that Tottenham wanted to buy him, he could hardly contain his excitement. It was even the same top Premier League club that his old Hamburg teammate, Rafael, had played for. They had spent hours together, talking about his time in England. Now, it was his turn – what an opportunity! Yes, Son Heung-min was also looking forward to living in a big city like London, but football still always came first. He loved Tottenham's tactics, their energetic style, and he was sure that working with a top coach like Pochettino would improve him as a player.

'Let's do this!' he told his agent eagerly.

So, on 28 August 2015, Son Heung-min signed

for Tottenham for a fee of £22 million, making him
the most expensive Asian footballer ever. Wow, that
was a lot to live up to, and he wouldn't even have a
preseason to help him settle in at his new club in a
new country. No, as he stood there smiling for the
cameras, proudly wearing the club's white shirt, the
new Premier League campaign had already begun.

'I'm looking forward to performing for the Spurs
fans as soon as possible,' he told the journalists. 'Bold
and daring – that's how I like to play.'

But away from the spotlight, Son Heung-min
was feeling nervous as well as excited. At last, his
childhood dream was about to come true, but what if
it turned out to be a disaster?

'I really need to start scoring straight away,' he
admitted to his parents, who had come to London
to live with him.

Although Son Heung-min had learned lots from
Ruud and Rafael about playing in the Premier League,
nothing could quite prepare him for the speed and
the physicality. On his debut, he struggled to get
into the game, or away from Sunderland's big, strong

centre-backs.

'Hey, surely that's a foul!' Son Heung-min thought as he fell to the floor once again, but no, the referee waved play on. He would just have to adapt to the more aggressive defending in England.

After sixty minutes, a few poor set pieces and one scuffed shot, Pochettino decided that he'd seen enough of his new signing.

'Welcome to English football,' he said with a smile. 'Don't worry, you'll get used to it, I promise!'

Son Heung-min feared that he might have wasted his one major chance to impress his new manager, but after scoring two goals in the Europa League against Qarabağ, he was back in the starting line-up for the next Premier League game against Crystal Palace. And this time, he made the most of his opportunity. It was still 0–0 midway through the second half, when he raced up the left wing onto Christian Eriksen's through-pass.

Taking the ball in his stride, Son Heung-min did what he did best, what had worked so well for him at Hamburg and Leverkusen – he dribbled his way into the box at top speed. The Palace defenders backed away, too scared to try and tackle him in case they gave away a penalty. The best they could do was keep him out wide on his left foot, which they assumed was weaker...

BANG! It wasn't one of Son Heung-min's greatest strikes, but luckily he'd put enough power on it to send it through the keeper's legs. *1–0!*

Gooooooooooooooooooooaaaaaaaaaaaaaaaalllllllllllllll llllllllllll!!!!!!!!!!!!!!!!!!!!

As the keeper lay there cursing his mistake, Son Heung-min was off, racing away to celebrate with the biggest smile on his face. All around White Hart Lane, the fans went wild, and it was all thanks to him.

'Well done, Sonny!' Christian cheered, putting an arm around his shoulders. 'Welcome to the club!'

Dele Alli was the next to arrive, followed by Harry and Erik. Soon, the only player missing was their goalkeeper, Hugo Lloris.

'Thanks, guys!' Son Heung-min said, beaming with joy. What a glorious moment! He was off the mark and he felt like part of the Tottenham team already.

CHAPTER 16

TOUGH TIMES AT TOTTENHAM

Sadly, after the high of scoring his first Premier League goal for Spurs, Son Heung-min soon came crashing back down to earth. Just days later, during the second half of his team's 4–1 thrashing of Manchester City, he picked up a painful injury and had to come off.

'Well played, Sonny – what happened to your foot?' Pochettino asked, giving him a pat on the back. 'We need you fit and firing!'

'Don't worry, I'm fine,' Son Heung-min replied, but the physio's report told a different story. He would need to rest for a few weeks to let his foot recover.

What terrible timing! In the end, Son Heung-min missed a whole month of football, including

Tottenham's Europa League matches against Monaco and Anderlecht, plus four Premier League games. At first, the team seemed to struggle without him, but those problems didn't last long. Harry, Dele, Erik, and Christian linked up brilliantly together as Tottenham won 5–1 against Bournemouth, and then 3–1 against Aston Villa.

'Oh no, I'm going to lose my starting spot!' Son Heung-min thought sadly.

Yes, it seemed that by the time he was ready to return, Tottenham's attack was playing so well in the Premier League that there was only space for him on the subs bench. At first, he stayed positive. Oh well, he would just have to keep working hard and wait for another chance to start...

As the weeks went by, however, the situation stayed the same. Son Heung-min scored in three Europa League games in a row, but he was still struggling to find his best form in the Premier League. And even when he came on and scored a last-minute winner against Watford, he couldn't change his manager's mind. Tottenham were in the Top Four, where they wanted to be, so Pochettino stuck with his successful starting XI. For the next match against Everton, Son Heung-min found himself back on the bench.

'At this rate, I'm never going to become a Premier League star!' he grumbled as his frustrations grew.

By February 2016, Tottenham weren't just aiming for a Top Four finish; no, they were chasing Leicester City for the title. With the pressure on, Pochettino needed attackers who were going to score, and not Son Heung-min, who was still stuck on only two goals in twenty-five Premier League games. He couldn't bear to look at the shocking stats; he was so much better than that! But after a promising start, his first season in England had become a nightmare.

It wasn't over yet, though. With three league games to go, another huge chance arrived. Dele was suspended for Spurs' must-win match against Chelsea, so Son Heung-min returned to the starting line-up. What an amazing opportunity to turn things around!

Moments before half-time, Christian slipped a beautiful pass through to Son Heung-min just as he made his favourite move, bursting between the

defenders and into the box. This was it; he wasn't
going to get a better chance to score. He took a touch
to steady himself and then slid the ball past the keeper.
2–0 to Tottenham!

*Goooooooooooooooooooooaaaaaaaaaaaaaaaaaallllllllllllllll
lllllllllllll!!!!!!!!!!!!!!!!!!!!!!*

Yes, he had done it; he had scored his third Premier
League goal at last and it was a very important one for
his team! As he celebrated with Harry and Erik, the
smile was finally back on Son Heung-min's face.

Unfortunately, however, that smile didn't last long.
In the second half, Gary Cahill got Chelsea back into
the game and suddenly, Spurs looked shaky. When
Son Heung-min was subbed off in the sixty-fifth
minute, his team were still winning 2–1, but in the
end, Eden Hazard scored an equaliser. As he watched
the goal go in, Son Heung-min's heart sank. A draw
wasn't enough; Tottenham's title dream was over.

After that disappointment, the rest of their season
really fizzled out. Despite another goal from Son
Heung-min, Spurs lost 2–1 at home to Southampton.
Then, on the final day of the season, they were

thrashed 5–1 away at Newcastle. Their performance was so poor that Pochettino decided to make two substitutions at half-time:

Tom Carroll on for Ryan Mason,

And Josh Onomah on for... Son Heung-min.

It was one of the most horrible and humiliating moments of his whole career. 'Why me?' he wanted to ask his manager, but instead, he stared down at the floor and kept quiet. It felt like his time at Tottenham was coming to an end already, after only one year. Maybe English football just wasn't for him.

That summer, Son Heung-min thought long and hard about his future. Did he really fit in at Spurs, or would he need to go somewhere else to succeed? Eventually, after long discussions with his parents, he made up his mind and told Spurs' manager:

'Gaffer, I want to go back to Germany.'

Pochettino wasn't surprised to hear Son Heung-min say that. He understood that it had been a frustrating first season for the forward. He hadn't played as often as he had hoped, and he had found it hard to adapt to a new country and a new style of football.

However, the Tottenham manager didn't want to let his £22-million signing leave just yet.

'Look, I know this year has been tough, but be patient and things will get better, I promise. I want you to stay and fight for your place. I believe in you – soon, you'll be a Premier League superstar.'

'Thanks, Coach!'

Son Heung-min went away from that meeting feeling much more positive. Now that he knew that he had his manager's support, he would stay and keep working hard until he achieved his aim of becoming a Tottenham hero.

CHAPTER 17

BACK WITH
A BANG!

The Tottenham counter-attack started slowly but it picked up speed as Dele passed the ball out wide to Christian. With a clever piece of skill, he dribbled inside, past the first Stoke City defender, and then looked up for a teammate in the middle.

'Yes!' Son Heung-min called out. He was standing unmarked near the penalty spot and with a delicate flick of his left foot, he guided Christian's cross into the bottom corner. *1–0!*

Gooooooooooooooooooooaaaaaaaaaaaaaaaalllllllllllllll llllllllllll!!!!!!!!!!!!!!!!!!

'Yesssss!' Son Heung-min shouted, punching the air with passion. It wasn't even half-time in his first

Premier League game of the 2016–17 season, and he was already back with a bang.

Early in the second half, Christian set up Son Heung-min again as he entered the Stoke City area. With his confidence up, he didn't even take a touch to control it. With a whip of his right foot, he curled the ball into the top corner first time. *2–0!*

Goooooooooooooooooooooaaaaaaaaaaaaaaaallllllllllllll lllllllllllll!!!!!!!!!!!!!!!!!!!

It was a magnificent strike, and he made it look so easy. With his arms out wide like an aeroplane, Son Heung-min weaved his way happily over to the corner flag and then waited for his teammates to arrive.

'Sonny, you're on fire!' Dele cheered as they did their special handshake together.

New season, new Son Heung-min – there was no stopping him now. He completed his brilliant comeback by setting up Harry for a simple tap-in. 4–0!

Job done! If he kept performing like that, Pochettino would have no choice but to pick him for every Premier League match...

Harry was out injured for Tottenham's away trip

to Middlesbrough, but for once, they didn't really miss their top striker. That's because up stepped Son Heung-min to score both goals for his team.

First, he burst into the box, dribbled past two defenders, and fired the ball in with his left foot. *1–0!*

Then, fifteen minutes later, he fought his way into the area again and scored with his right foot instead. *2–0!*

'Wow Sonny, I'm so glad you stayed!' Jan Vertonghen shouted, giving him a big bear hug.

'Me too!' Son Heung-min replied. After just three games, he had already equalled last season's total of four Premier League goals!

'He's a different person now,' Pochettino proclaimed.

Yes, Son Heung-min was back to being the confident, positive player he used to be, full of energy and self-belief. It had taken him a long time and a lot of tough training sessions to adapt, but now he finally felt settled in the Premier League. Just like in his early days at Hamburg, he had learned and improved, and with his manager's support, he had completely turned things around. Only a few months earlier, he had been subbed off at half-time against Newcastle – but now he was Tottenham's top scorer!

Son Heung-min's sensational form continued in the Champions League against CKSA Moscow. His first scoring chance arrived early in the second half, when the ball landed at his feet just outside the penalty area. He struck it first time towards the bottom corner, but unfortunately, it flew just wide of the post.

'So close!' Son Heung-min groaned, lifting his hands to his face. When he was playing this well, he expected to score every time. Never mind, he wouldn't waste the next chance...

In the seventieth minute, Son Heung-min timed his run to perfection to beat the offside trap and race through one-on-one with the CSKA keeper. It wasn't one of his best finishes, but it was good enough to squeeze the ball just past the keeper. *1–0!*

Goooooooooooooooooooaaaaaaaaaaaaaaaaalllllllllllllll llllllllllll!!!!!!!!!!!!!!!!!!!

With an excited dance, Son Heung-min ran over to celebrate with Christian. Another game, another winning goal – he had never felt so invincible! There was no time to stop and enjoy his success, though. No, Harry Kane was still out injured, and league leaders Manchester City were up next...

'Come on, we can win this!' their captain Hugo Lloris bellowed with belief as the players prepared for kick-off.

This time, Son Heung-min didn't manage to score himself, but he did create the second goal for Dele with an excellent, defence-splitting pass. He was now a key part of the Tottenham team, and with that 2–0 win, they moved just one point behind City at the top of the table.

What a start to the season! And to top it all off, Son Heung-min was also selected as the Premier League Player of the Month for September.

'This is my dream, to get the award,' he said, holding the trophy in his hands. Although he was proud of his achievement, he was already looking ahead. 'I want to win it a second time, a third time.'

Yes, Son Heung-min was now ready to take the next step and become a consistent performer, all season long. He was all set to become the Premier

League superstar that he had always wanted to be.

Harry, Dele, Christian, and Son Heung-min – with that fab front four all playing together, there were exciting times ahead for Tottenham.

CHAPTER 18

TOTTENHAM'S
FAB FRONT FOUR

Once Harry Kane returned to Tottenham in November 2016, it was only a matter of time before the team's front four hit top form together. And when it happened, poor Swansea City didn't stand a chance.

First, Dele won a penalty, which Harry scored. *1–0!*

After that, the Tottenham attack had the freedom and confidence to play their best, flowing football. They all got on really well together and it showed in their teamwork on the pitch.

Harry dummied the ball, letting it run through to Dele, who laid it back to Christian. His shot was blocked, but the rebound fell to Son Heung-min, who fired it in with an acrobatic finish. *2–0!*

And the next goal was even better, featuring a beautiful display of one-touch passing. Harry back to Christian, Christian forward to Dele, Dele across to Son Heung-min. Tottenham made attacking look so easy and exciting. *ZOOM!* He sprinted into the Swansea box, but just as he was about to shoot, he left it for Harry to strike. *3–0!*

What a great team goal! And Tottenham's fab front four weren't finished yet.

Dele's shot looped up off the keeper and Christian was there to head it in. *4–0!*

In the final seconds, Christian scored again. *5–0!*

With that amazing attacking performance, Spurs sent out a warning to the rest of the Premier League – Beware, Fab Front Four Here! It didn't make them any easier to defend against, though.

Christian scored two against Hull,

Dele scored two against Southampton,

Dele and Harry scored two each against Watford,

And Harry scored a hat-trick against West Brom.

But what about Son Heung-min? Well, he was still playing an important role, even if he wasn't scoring as many Premier League goals as Tottenham's other attackers. And in the FA Cup, he was his team's main man:

One against Aston Villa,

Two against Wycombe Wanderers,

And Three against Millwall.

Yes, with a last-minute volley that squirmed through the keeper's legs, Son Heung-min completed his first Spurs hat-trick! Lifting both arms up in the air like a champion, he held up three fingers on each hand.

'Nice one, Sonny!' Christian cheered.

Starring against Millwall was one thing, but could he be the hero against Manchester City, when his team needed him most? In the Premier League, Tottenham were trailing 2–1 away at their title rivals, with fifteen minutes to go, when Son Heung-min stepped up and showed what a big game player he could be. Christian crossed the ball, Harry flicked it on, and there was Son Heung-min, unmarked in the middle, to fire a fierce, first-time shot into the bottom corner. *2–2!*

Goooooooooooooooooooooaaaaaaaaaaaaaaaaalllllllllllllll llllllllllll!!!!!!!!!!!!!!!!!!!!

Son Heung-min slid towards the corner flag on his knees. Yes, he had saved the day for Spurs!

And there were even tougher tasks ahead. In April 2017, Harry was ruled out with another injury, and so Tottenham turned to Son Heung-min once again to be their top scorer. No problem!

GOAL! He tapped in at the back post against Burnley,

GOAL! He scored another against Swansea,

GOAL, GOAL! He grabbed one with each foot against Watford.

Those were Son Heung-min's tenth and eleventh league goals of the season, and how did he celebrate his achievement? By doing special handshakes with all of his teammates – and he had a different one for each of them!

'How do you remember all of them?' Dele asked and Son Heung-min shrugged. It was just part of being the friendliest, most popular player on the planet! With his football talent and winning smile, he wanted to bring happiness to as many people as possible.

And it was working – everyone loved him now. In his second season at Spurs, Son Heung-min had successfully become a fan favourite, as well as a top teammate. How? By scoring lots of great goals! Even when Harry came back from injury, he kept on firing.

GOAL! He burst into the box and nutmegged the Bournemouth keeper.

Five goals in four games! That was enough to win Son Heung-min his second Premier League Player of the Month award of the season. And more importantly, his goals helped Tottenham to win all four matches and stay on track to finish second behind Chelsea.

Although they weren't going to win the Premier League title this time, Spurs were making real progress under Pochettino. To prove it, their amazing attackers teamed up to thrash Leicester City.

Son Heung-min raced onto a through ball, before pulling it back for Harry to strike. *1–0!*

Dele chipped the ball over the defence for Son Heung-min to volley in. *2–0!*

'Yessss!' he yelled as he ran over to kiss the camera.

Harry headed the ball in from inside the six-yard box. *3–1!*

Son Heung-min sprinted forward on the counter-attack and his finishing was as accurate as ever. *4–1!*

Harry completed yet another hat-trick and then added a fourth – almost just for fun. *5–1, 6–1!*

After the final whistle, the two goalscorers walked around the pitch together with their arms around each other. Job done; Leicester destroyed – what a dangerous duo they were! No wonder the supporters were so excited about their team and their chances of winning a trophy.

Glory, Glory Tottenham Hotspur,
And the Spurs go marching on, on, on!!!

As his second year at the club came to an end, Son Heung-min looked back with pride and then forward with positivity. Twenty-one goals and nine assists – what an improvement on his previous numbers! That was more like it from a £22-million man. But even after his best-ever season, he still believed that he could do better.

CHAPTER 19

MAKING HISTORY AND HUNGRY FOR MORE

Nice one, Sonny, nice one Son,
Nice one, Sonny, let's have another one!

Tottenham were off to a dream start at their new
home for the 2017-18 season, Wembley Stadium.
Moments after giving his team the lead against
Liverpool, Harry Kane collected Hugo Lloris's long
throw and dribbled over the halfway line. Did he have
the speed to go all the way himself and score? No, but
he knew someone who did...

ZOOM! As soon as his feet touched the centre-
circle, Son Heung-min was off, sprinting forward as
fast as he could. James Milner and Jordan Henderson

did their best to keep up, but they had no chance of catching him.

'Yes!' Son Heung-min cried out and Harry's pass was perfect. So perfect, that he didn't even need to take a touch before calmly placing the ball past the keeper. *2–0!*

Gooooooooooooooooooaaaaaaaaaaaaaaaalllllllllllll llllllllllll!!!!!!!!!!!!!!!!!!!

The astonishing speed, the accurate shot – it was another classic Son Heung-min strike. As he jogged over to the corner flag, he beamed his biggest smile and blew kisses to the Tottenham supporters in the stands. He loved them, and these days, they loved him right back. They even had their own special song for him:

Nice one, Sonny, nice one Son,

Nice one, Sonny, let's have another one!

Although he didn't score another one against Liverpool, he did two weeks later against Crystal Palace, and what a magnificent and momentous goal it was. As the second half ticked by, the score remained 0–0. A draw wouldn't do. Tottenham needed to win to stay in the Premier League title race. But despite dominating the game, they were struggling to get past the stubborn Palace defence.

Come On, You Spurs!

Harry thought about taking another shot, but he was surrounded by red-and-blue shirts, so he passed it left to Danny Rose instead. His shot was blocked and then moments later, Moussa Sissoko's cross was cleared. It was impossible; there was no way through! It looked like it was going to be a very frustrating Sunday afternoon for Spurs, unless a hero could save the day...

As the ball bounced towards him on the edge of the box, Son Heung-min kept his cool and took control of the situation. Shifting it onto his left foot, he curled a shot past five Palace defenders and one desperately diving keeper. *1–0!*

Gooooooooooooooooooooaaaaaaaaaaaaaaaaaalllllllllllllll lllllllllllll!!!!!!!!!!!!!!!!!!!

Son Heung-min celebrated like a true superstar:

The arms-out aeroplane,

Followed by the running kneeslide,

And finally, the passionate double fist-pump.

'Sonny, what a strike!' Moussa shouted, hugging him tightly.

Not only was Son Heung-min the matchwinner, but he was also now a record-breaker. That was his twentieth goal, taking him ahead of his childhood hero, Park Ji-sung, as the leading Asian scorer in Premier League history.

After the game, however, Son Heung-min was as humble and hungry as ever. 'I have broken the record, but I still have a long way to go to catch Park,' he told the journalists from South Korea. 'I scored, but good players do more than that.'

Yes, what Son Heung-min wanted more than goals was his first team trophy. Park Ji-sung had won two league titles at PSV, and then four more at Manchester United, plus three League Cups and the Champions League. Son Heung-min still had a long way to go to reach that level, but he had to start somewhere. So, could Tottenham finally lift some silverware, after ten long years of waiting? That was Pochettino's plan.

'Come on, we can do this!' he urged his players on.

So, which trophy would they win?

The League Cup, like they won in 2008? No, Spurs lost to West Ham in the Fourth Round, despite Son Heung-min scoring twice.

The Champions League? No, Spurs lost to Juventus in the Last 16, despite Son Heung-min giving them the lead in the second leg. Moments after missing a glorious chance, he was back in the box, lifting the ball over Gianluigi Buffon.

Goooooooooooooooooooooaaaaaaaaaaaaaaaaaalllllllllllllll lllllllllllll!!!!!!!!!!!!!!!!!!!!!

'Yesssss!' Son Heung-min cried out on his knees as all around him Wembley went wild. But sadly, it wasn't to be for Spurs, as Juventus fought back in the second half to win.

The Premier League? No, Spurs finished third, a massive twenty-three points behind leaders Manchester City, despite another very solid season. Harry was their top scorer with thirty goals, but who was second? Son Heung-min, with twelve! There had been so many magical moments:

The run and strike against Stoke City,

The long-range rocket against West Ham,

The diving header against Huddersfield…

And thanks to those goals, Son Heung-min had made history again. He became the first Asian player ever to finish in the Top Ten scorers in a Premier League season. But although he was proud of his achievement, what he really wanted was a trophy.

The FA Cup? This was it – Tottenham's last chance to win a trophy in 2018. But no, despite Son Heung-min's two assists against Newport County and two goals against Rochdale, his team ended up losing in the semi-finals.

'Not again!' Son Heung-min muttered to himself as he walked off the pitch at Wembley. It was the same old story for Spurs and their talented team – they kept getting so close to glory, but in the end, it was yet another season without a trophy.

Son Heung-min was desperate to give the Tottenham supporters something to celebrate, but for now, that aim would have to wait. Because the 2018 World Cup was only days away, and his country was counting on him.

CHAPTER 20

SUCCESS WITH SOUTH KOREA AT LAST!

So, four years on from their disappointing display in Brazil, could South Korea come back stronger at the 2018 World Cup? Ki Sung-yueng was back, this time as captain, and so were Koo Ja-cheol and Kim Young-gwon. But there was no doubt about the team's most important player: their Premier League superstar, Son Heung-min. Could he shine on the international stage and shoot the Taegeuk Warriors to World Cup success once again?

Son Heung-min really hoped so because time was running out for him to escape from military duty. He would soon turn twenty-six and in South Korea, all males had to do two years of national service before the age of twenty-eight. Two years?! That was a lot of time to miss, especially when a football career was so short. There was only one way that Son Heung-min could avoid it: by helping the national team to achieve something of real significance, like reaching the World Cup semi-finals, as The Taegeuk Warriors had in 2002.

Or winning the Asian Cup. But unfortunately, despite Son Heung-min's goal, South Korea had lost to Australia in the final in 2015.

Or winning an Olympic medal. But unfortunately, they had suffered a surprise defeat to Honduras in the quarter-finals in 2016.

The next target for South Korea was World Cup success, but it wasn't going to be easy at all. First, they would have to get through a really tough group, featuring Sweden, Mexico, and the World Champions, Germany. And even if they achieved that, there would be lots more amazing opponents ahead, teams packed with world-class players. While South Korea were a very well-organised side, they relied heavily on their one superstar.

So, was Son Heung-min starting to feel the pressure?

No – as usual, he only saw the positive side of being his country's most famous and popular player. 'I'm such a lucky guy,' he said with a humble smile.

First up: Sweden. There was no Zlatan Ibrahimović these days, but they were still a very solid team, especially in defence. Son Heung-min and his fellow attackers only had two shots all game, and neither of them hit the target. But just when the match looked like it was heading for a dull 0–0 draw, Kim Min-woo challenged Viktor Claesson in the South Korea box.

'Penalty!' the Sweden players screamed at the referee.

Son Heung-min got the ball and tried to play on, but after checking with VAR, the spot-kick was awarded. 1–0 to Sweden, and it stayed that way until the final whistle.

It was the worst possible start for South Korea, and for Son Heung-min. As he trudged off the pitch, his head hung low with disappointment. He had failed to even create one single chance! That was his responsibility and he had let his country down.

'I feel very, very sorry for my teammates because if we don't score, it's my fault,' Son Heung-min told the national newspapers. He was determined to do better in the next match.

Mexico, however, proved too strong for South Korea. In the last minute, Son Heung-min curled a stunning left-foot strike into the bottom corner, but by then, his team had already lost the game and their tournament was all but over.

Son Heung-min did his best to hide his emotions as he shook hands with the Mexico players out on the pitch, but by the time he entered the dressing room, he was in a flood of tears again. Four years on from their embarrassing defeat to Algeria, and it felt like South Korea hadn't improved at all!

They still had one more game to go, though – against Germany. It was their last chance to give the South Korean people something to cheer about.

'Come on, let's show them what we can do!' Son Heung-min said, wearing the captain's armband with pride.

And the players listened to their new leader. They defended heroically – blocking, tackling, heading, clearing every ball. Then, as the Germans grew more and more frustrated, the Taegeuk Warriors pushed forward on the counter-attack.

Son Heung-min's low corner-kick bounced all the way through the six-yard box until it reached Kim Young-gwon at the back post.

'Yesss!' Son Heung-min cheered, throwing his arms up in the air, but not for long. The linesman's flag was up – offside.

'No way, that came off a German player last!' the South Koreans protested, and they were right. After an anxious wait for the VAR decision, they got their goal. *1–0 to South Korea!*

'YESSS!' Son Heung-min cheered again, louder this time, as he jumped into his teammates' arms. It was a massive moment for his country, and there was even better to come.

As soon as Ju Se-jong stole the ball off Germany's keeper, Manuel Neuer, he launched it forward straight away. He knew that his captain would be waiting. *ZOOM!* Son Heung-min was off, sprinting away from Niklas Süle in a flash, before passing the ball into the empty net. *2–0!*

*Goooooooooooooooooooooaaaaaaaaaaaaaaaaallllllllllllll
llllllllllll!!!!!!!!!!!!!!!!!!!*

What a way to end his 2018 World Cup! Standing
in front of the supporters, Son Heung-min gave the
badge on his shirt a passionate kiss. Starring for his
country meant so, so much to him.

The South Korea players left Russia with their heads
held high. After all, they had just beaten the World
Champions 2–0! It was exactly the kind of confidence
boost that the Taegeuk Warriors needed ahead of their
second tournament of the summer – the Asian Games.

Although it was mainly an Under-23s competition,
each team could select three over-age players. For
South Korea, those three were:

Goalkeeper Jo Hyeon-woo,

Forward Hwang Ui-jo,

And superstar captain Son Heung-min!

Son Heung-min couldn't wait to lead his team to
victory. If they could return to South Korea with the
trophy in their hands, then surely the government
wouldn't make him do military service anymore? Son
Heung-min crossed his fingers and got ready to shine.

GOAL! He scored the winner against Kyrgyzstan to get them out of the group stage.

ASSIST, ASSIST! He set up two goals for Hwang Ui-jo as they beat Uzbekistan in the quarter-finals.

ASSIST! He poked another clever pass through to Hwang Ui-jo as they beat Vietnam in the semi-finals.

Son Heung-min and his teammates were now just one win away from glory! The trophy wasn't theirs yet, though; no, first they would have to beat their big rivals, Japan.

'Come on, Sonny – you can do it!'

The whole of South Korea was behind him, plus every Tottenham supporter too. They definitely didn't want to lose one of the best players for two whole years!

But after ninety minutes of football, the score was still 0–0. Which team would win it in extra-time, or would the final go all the way to penalties?

'Noooooo!' After a long season with Tottenham, followed by a long summer with South Korea, Son Heung-min was absolutely exhausted, but there was no way he was giving up now. He wasn't going to waste such a big chance to win a trophy.

'Let's win this!' he urged his teammates as they took to the field again.

In extra-time, Son Heung-min really led by example. He was everywhere – winning the ball in midfield and launching attack after attack. Surely, South Korea would score...

As Son Heung-min cut in from the left wing, he thought about going for goal himself, but instead he left it for Lee Seung-woo. It turned out to be a wise decision because the midfielder blasted the ball beautifully into the top corner of the net. *1–0!*

At last, South Korea were winning! And eight minutes later, Son Heung-min set up his team's second goal too. He floated a free kick to the back post, where Hwang Hee-chan jumped highest to head it home. *2–0!*

Japan did pull one goal back, but it wasn't enough. At the final whistle, South Korea were the winners! In that moment, Son Heung-min's tiredness seemed to disappear. 'No more military service!' he thought, breathing a sigh of relief. He raced around the pitch, smiling, hugging, and lifting his teammates into the air.

'We did it, we did it!'

This time, there were tears of pride and joy, rather than pain and disappointment. Son Heung-min ran over to the sea of red supporters to celebrate, with a national flag in each hand. What a fantastic feeling it was to achieve success with South Korea at last!

CHAPTER 21

CHALLENGING FOR THE CHAMPIONS LEAGUE

Son Heung-min had won his first international trophy at last, but that didn't satisfy him. No, after that first taste of glory, he was hungry for more. Surely, Tottenham were too good a team to go yet another season without silverware?

It took Son Heung-min a few weeks to recover from his busy summer of 2018 with South Korea, but once he did, he was soon back to his best:

GOAL! He weaved his way through the Chelsea defence, before firing a shot past the keeper.

GOAL! He curled another left-foot cracker into the top corner against Leicester City.

He scored two more against Everton, then two

more against Bournemouth.

GOAL! He blasted a rebound into the Watford net.

GOAL! He popped up with a late winner to break Newcastle hearts.

Son Heung-min was on fire, with eleven goals in his last thirteen league games! He was now only three behind Harry as his team's top scorer. But despite his best efforts, Tottenham couldn't keep up with Manchester City and Liverpool at the top of the Premier League table.

'Not again!' Son Heung-min groaned as they slipped to a 2–1 defeat at Burnley.

It was the same old story, and Spurs had also been knocked out of both the League Cup and the FA Cup, while Son Heung-min was away playing for South Korea at the Asian Cup. That meant there was only one trophy left for Tottenham to win, and it was the toughest of them all: the Champions League.

After a slow start to the competition, Son Heung-min and his teammates had really turned things around. With a hard-fought draw at Barcelona, they had squeezed through the group stage, before cruising comfortably past Borussia Dortmund in the Round of 16. Ever since his days at Hamburg, Son Heung-min had always loved playing against the Germans, and he scored once again with a stunning side-foot volley.

Goooooooooooooooooooooaaaaaaaaaaaaaaaaalllllllllllllll lllllllllllll!!!!!!!!!!!!!!!!!!!!!

'Yesssss!' Son Heung-min cried out to the supporters after doing his special handshake with Serge Aurier.

Tottenham were through to the Champions League quarter-finals for the first time since 2011. It was a clear sign of the progress they were making, but it would mean nothing if their journey ended there, against their English rivals, Manchester City.

'Come on, we can beat them!' Pochettino urged his players on. 'Be brave, and show no fear!'

It was only Tottenham's second match at their brand-new stadium, and who had scored the first goal to win the first game there? Son Heung-min, of course! So, could he do it again, when it mattered most, on a big European night, in front of 60,000 fans?

Yes, he could! With fifteen minutes to go and Harry off injured, Son Heung-min raced into the Manchester

City box to reach Christian's pass. His first touch wasn't as good as it normally was, but he didn't give up. He used his speed to get to the ball just before it went off the pitch.

'Ref, that's a goal kick!'

While the City players stood there appealing, Son Heung-min took full advantage. In a flash, he dribbled inside, past Fabian Delph, and fired a fierce shot past Ederson. *1–0!*

Goooooooooooooooooooooaaaaaaaaaaaaaaaalllllllllllllll llllllllllll!!!!!!!!!!!!!!!!!!!!

What a noise, what a feeling! He was the hero again at the Tottenham Hotspur Stadium. For once, however, Son Heung-min wasn't smiling. He had his serious, game-face on because it wasn't over yet.

'Focus!' he called out to his teammates as the game kicked off again.

Tottenham held on and headed to the Etihad Stadium with a 1–0 advantage. So, would they sit back, defend deep and protect their lead? No, what followed was one of the most exciting matches that Son Heung-min had ever played in.

Within four minutes, Raheem Sterling had already made it 1–1 on aggregate, so Spurs had no choice but to try and score. Lucas Moura dribbled forward and played it to Dele, who tried to slip a pass through to Christian. A City defender blocked it, but the ball fell straight to Son Heung-min on the edge of the box. He wasn't going to miss from there. *BANG!*

Goooooooooooooooooooooaaaaaaaaaaaaaaaallllllllllllll llllllllllll!!!!!!!!!!!!!!!!!!!!!

And three mad minutes later, Son Heung-min scored again. Lucas stole the ball off Aymeric Laporte and launched another quick counter-attack. As he approached the penalty area, he laid it back to Christian, who passed it on to his team's sharpest shooter. *BANG!*

It was a strike that Son Heung-min had practised a million times before, even during his early days training with his father back in South Korea. There was only going to be one outcome:

Goooooooooooooooooooooaaaaaaaaaaaaaaaallllllllllllll llllllllllll!!!!!!!!!!!!!!!!!!!!!

It was now 3–1 to Tottenham on aggregate, and

Son Heung-min looked unstoppable! So, however, did Manchester City's attackers.

Bernardo Silva's shot deflected past Hugo. *3–2!*

And before half-time, Sterling scored again. *3–3!*

What a weird and wonderful game! Things did calm down a bit in the second half, but there were still more goals to come.

The first went to City, scored by Sergio Agüero. *4–3!*

And the second? It went to Spurs, scored by Fernando Llorente, in the strangest way. Kieran Trippier's corner-kick bounced off his hip and into the City net. After a nervous wait for VAR, the goal was given: *4–4!*

Tottenham were winning again, but only on away goals! And there was still time for one more big, dramatic moment. In stoppage time, Bernardo Silva intercepted Christian's pass and flicked it forward to Agüero, who squared it to Raheem, who fired a shot past Hugo. *5–4 to City!*

Or was it? It wasn't time for the Tottenham players to despair just yet because VAR was taking a look at a possible offside...

'NO GOAL' – as the words flashed up on the big screen, Son Heung-min felt like celebrating, but no, that would have to wait. They still had a few more minutes of defending to do first.

But soon, it was all over – Tottenham were through to the Champions League semi-finals!

'Sonny, you're a hero!' Lucas shouted, throwing his arms around his teammate. Yes, with two goals and another tireless performance, Son Heung-min had certainly played a crucial part in his team's success. It was the greatest game of his entire career.

'I have never seen something like this,' he admitted in an interview after the match. 'It was madness.'

After that wild win over Manchester City, the Tottenham players were hoping for a quiet, simple semi-final against Ajax, but it wasn't to be. With Son Heung-min suspended and Harry still injured, they lost the first leg 1–0 at home. Uh-oh, Spurs had some serious work to do now.

And at half-time in Amsterdam, it really looked like game over. Tottenham now needed to score at least three goals in order to make it through to the final.

Impossible? No, they were a team who never gave up.

Dele set up Lucas, who raced through and scored. *3–1!*

Son Heung-min passed to Kieran who crossed it to Fernando. It looked like a certain goal, but somehow he missed. Not to worry, though – the rebound fell to Lucas who weaved his way through to score again. *3–2!*

Unbelievable! Could Tottenham complete an incredible comeback and win on away goals again?

In the final seconds, Fernando knocked a long ball down to Dele, who flicked it through to Lucas again. His shot rolled past the keeper and into the bottom corner. *3–3!*

This time, it was Son Heung-min's turn to throw his arms around his teammate. 'Lucas, you're a hero!' he shouted at the end of another exciting night in Europe. Against all odds, Tottenham were through to their first-ever Champions final!

After such an amazing adventure to get there, and all the hours of pre-game build-up, the final itself was sadly a big disappointment. Tottenham were losing 1–0 to Liverpool before Son Heung-min had even touched the ball! And this time, they never really recovered.

Christian blasted a shot high over the bar,

Dele's chip landed comfortably in Alisson's gloves, and when Son Heung-min tried to sprint through the defence, Virgil van Dijk was there to stop him.

It was no use; even when Son Heung-min finally found the space to strike one of his most thunderous shots, the Liverpool keeper dived down to save it.

'Noooo!' he groaned with his hands on his head.

Once more, Tottenham had come so close to glory, but in the end, it was another season without a trophy. As he walked sadly up onto the stage to collect his medal, Son Heung-min felt so fed up and frustrated. They had worked so hard all year, and for what?

The next day, however, his normal positivity returned. Son Heung-min looked back with pride on what his team had achieved so far, and then forward to the future. He would never give up on his Tottenham trophy dream; he was determined to go again.

CHAPTER 22

MOURINHO'S MAIN MAN

Despite Son Heung-min's determination, Tottenham made a poor start to the 2019–20 Premier League season. He helped his team to beat Crystal Palace and Southampton, but they lost to Newcastle, Leicester, and Brighton. With ten games played, they were way down in eleventh place, already sixteen points behind the League leaders, Liverpool.

As the bad results continued, the Spurs supporters were growing more and more restless. Instead of moving closer to winning a trophy, their team was slipping further away! Something had to change, and the club chairman, Daniel Levy, decided that it was the manager. So, after five years at Tottenham,

Pochettino was replaced by former Chelsea and Manchester United boss, José Mourinho.

Yes, the times were changing at Tottenham, and many fans weren't happy about Levy's decision. There was no doubt that Mourinho was a very successful manager; after all, he had won the Premier League title three times, and the Champions League twice. But what about his style of play? Tottenham were known as an attacking team, whereas Mourinho preferred a very defensive approach, especially compared to Pochettino.

That was something that the players worried about too, especially the forwards like Son Heung-min. While he was sad to say goodbye to his old mentor Pochettino, he had to stay focused and think about his future. How would he fit into Spurs' new system? After working as hard as ever in training, he waited anxiously to see the teamsheet for Mourinho's first match against West Ham:

20 Dele Alli,

27 Lucas Moura,

10 Harry Kane...

…And 07 Son Heung-min.

Phew! He had made it into Mourinho's starting XI. Now, it was time for him to show that he deserved to stay there.

By the time Harry Winks's pass landed at Dele's feet, Son Heung-min was already running towards the box. And as he turned, Dele knew exactly where to find his teammate: in the gap between the West Ham right-back and centre-back. PING!

When the ball arrived, Son Heung-min still had Issa Diop to beat, but with a double stepover, he created enough space to shoot with his lethal left. *BANG!*

Gooooooooooooooooooooaaaaaaaaaaaaaaalllllllllllllll llllllllllll!!!!!!!!!!!!!!!!!!!!

'Yesssss!' Son Heung-min yelled as he jumped up and punched the air. What a start! It was the perfect way to impress his new manager.

And just before half-time, he helped to double Tottenham's lead. Collecting Dele's clever flick-on, Son Heung-min sprinted up the left wing, before delivering a beautiful cross to Lucas. *2–0!*

Early in the second half, Harry scored a third and

Tottenham were looking like a top attacking team again. Mourinho was off the mark with a debut win and he was delighted with his players, especially Son Heung-min.

'I am already in love with this guy,' the new Tottenham manager told the media. 'He's a fantastic player.'

Suddenly, everything was going right for Son Heung-min. A few days later, he received the Asian International Player of the Year award for the third time in his career. And on the pitch for Tottenham, his terrific performances continued. He provided assists for Dele and Moussa against Bournemouth, and then dribbled all the way from the edge of his own box against Burnley! It was the kind of wondergoal that the Brazilian striker Ronaldo used to score and so Mourinho gave his star man a new nickname: 'Sonaldo'.

No wonder Son Heung-min was feeling full of confidence as Spurs prepared to take on London rivals Chelsea at the Tottenham Hotspur Stadium. But as the game went on, his self-belief faded, and his frustration grew.

'Why did no-one close him down?' he moaned as Willian made it 1–0.

'Nooo, what was that?!' he groaned as he skied a shot high and wide.

'What a disaster!' he muttered as Willian scored a second from the penalty spot.

But in fact, the worst part was still to come. Midway through the second half, Son Heung-min controlled a long pass from Jan Vertonghen, and as he turned to pass to Dele, the Chelsea defender Antonio Rüdiger fouled him deliberately.

'Hey!' Son Heung-min shouted angrily, and as he landed on the grass, he kicked out, sending Rüdiger flying to the floor too.

'Come on, he's faking – it was an accident anyway!' he tried to tell the referee, but Anthony Taylor wasn't so sure. After checking with VAR, he went to his pocket and pulled out a... RED CARD!

Son Heung-min was so shocked to be sent off that he collapsed to his knees, covering his face with his hands. No way, he was one of the good guys! Surely, the referee had got it wrong! But there was nothing he could do about it now. As well as missing the rest of the match, he would also be suspended for the next three games.

Oh well – all Son Heung-min could do was accept his punishment and come back stronger. He returned just in time to replace Harry Kane, who had picked up another injury. His team needed him more than ever and Son Heung-min was determined not to let them down. There would be no more mistakes and no more key chances missed. No, from now on, he would be a cool, calm scoring machine, Mourinho's main man.

GOAL! He headed home the winner against Norwich.

GOAL! He scored Spurs' second against Manchester City.

GOAL! He saved the day against Aston Villa, with a last-minute solo run.

At the final whistle, there was good news and bad news for Son Heung-min. The good news was that he had just set a new record by becoming the first Asian player ever to score fifty Premier League goals. Another proud achievement! The bad news, however, was that his season might well be over. He had hurt his arm in the very first minute of the game and despite playing on until the end, the doctor's scan showed a serious bone fracture.

'Noooooo!' Son Heung-min groaned, thinking of all the important matches he was going to miss: Chelsea away, Manchester United at home, and biggest of all, the North London derby against Arsenal. Without him and Harry, who was going to step up and score the winning goals for Spurs?

The answer was: 'no-one'. Son Heung-min could hardly bear to watch as his team lost to Chelsea and Wolves in the Premier League, and then to RB Leipzig in the Champions League. Noooo, what a disaster!

After that, however, the season had to be suspended due to COVID-19. Some things were far more important than football, especially people's health.

'Stay safe,' Son Heung-min posted on Instagram to his millions of followers around the world, along with photos of him exercising at home.

Yes, while the players waited, wondering if and when the season would continue, Son Heung-min was working as hard as ever. In fact, as soon as his arm had healed, he returned to South Korea to complete his military service, which had been reduced from two years to just three weeks. The training was tough and challenging, but Son Heung-min enjoyed the experience. By the end, he felt really fit, and even more excited about playing football again.

'Come onnnnn!' Son Heung-min cheered as the Premier League season restarted. It felt so good to be back in action alongside Harry in the Spurs attack. And soon, it was time for the big one: the North London derby.

Even though there were no fans allowed at the Tottenham Hotspur Stadium, any game against Arsenal was a must-win match. Son Heung-min had known that even before he arrived in England. However, in his five years at Spurs, he still hadn't scored a single goal against their local rivals. Well, it was time to change that.

Arsenal took the lead through Alexandre Lacazette, but Tottenham fought back straight away. When David Luiz slipped as he tried to control Sead Kolasinac's poor pass, Son Heung-min was there, ready to pounce. *ZOOM!* He used his speed to overtake Luiz and his strength to shrug him off. Then, as the keeper dived at his feet, Son Heung-min coolly chipped the ball over him and watched it roll into the back of the net. *1–1!*

Goooooooooooooooooooooaaaaaaaaaaaaaaaallllllllllllll llllllllllll!!!!!!!!!!!!!!!!!!!!!

At last, he had done it in the North London derby! Son Heung-min stopped to high-five Harry and Lucas, but there were no happy smiles… yet.

'We've got to win this now!' the Tottenham players agreed. But could they score a second?

Ben Davies hit the crossbar,

Son Heung-min stumbled in the six-yard box,

Harry's shot was saved,

But finally, the winning goal arrived. With ten minutes to go, Son Heung-min curled a perfect corner-kick onto Toby Alderweireld's head. *2–1 to Tottenham!*

'Yesssss!' Son Heung-min screamed, smiling this time. With a goal and an assist, he had won the North London derby for his team. What a hero! And Mourinho's main man was only just getting started.

CHAPTER 23

THE SON AND HARRY SHOW

Uh-oh – Spurs were in a spot of trouble again. As half-time approached, Mourinho's men were losing 1–0 away at Southampton. Two defeats out of two would be a terrible start to the 2020–21 season – they couldn't let that happen. But who was going to turn things around for Tottenham? Although Lucas Moura and Tanguy Ndombele both sometimes scored goals, the team really relied on their two star strikers.

'Yes, NOW!' Son Heung-min called out to Harry as he sprinted through the middle. They both knew that he was far too fast for the Southampton defenders.

It looked like Harry had overhit the pass, but no, Son Heung-min still reached it first, and with his right foot, he curled a shot into the far corner. *1–1!*

Goooooooooooooooooooooaaaaaaaaaaaaaaaaallllllllllllll llllllllllll!!!!!!!!!!!!!!!!!!

Tottenham's talented Number 7 punched the air with purpose – thanks to him, his team were back in the game! And as soon as the second half began, the Son and Harry Show continued. Their understanding was so strong that each of them knew exactly what the other would do next. It felt like every counter-attack led to a goal.

Harry turned and slipped the ball through to Son Heung-min. He burst past the centre-back and then fired an unstoppable left-foot shot past the keeper. *2–1!*

And fifteen minutes later, they linked up again. Son Heung-min raced onto Harry's pass and slid a shot through the keeper's legs. *3–1!*

HAT-TRICK! It was his second for Spurs, but his first in the Premier League. Son Heung-min smiled and held up three fingers as he ran over to celebrate with Harry.

'Thanks, H – you're the best!'

And Tottenham's deadly duo weren't done yet. Harry crossed the ball in from the right, knowing that his teammate would be there waiting. Son Heung-min chested it down and finished with the confidence of a hat-trick hero. *4–1!*

Four goals for Son Heung-min and four assists for Harry Kane – was there a more exciting strike partnership in the entire Premier League? No! And two weeks later, they put on another masterclass against Manchester United.

Harry's clever quick free kick set Son Heung-min through to score. *2–1!*

Son Heung-min could have shot himself, but he pulled it back to Harry instead. *3–1!*

Son Heung-min made a late run into the six-yard box to get on the end of Serge Aurier's cross. *4–1!*

Harry stepped up to score from the spot. *6–1!*

Two goals each at Old Trafford – what an impressive away performance! And Tottenham's star strikeforce didn't stop there; no, they kept scoring goal after goal:

Son Heung-min got one against West Ham and Harry got two,

Son Heung-min headed in the winner at Burnley,

and who had created it? Harry, of course!

With a 2–0 win over Manchester City, Tottenham moved to the top of the Premier League table, and who were their heroes yet again? Son Heung-min scored the first with an excellent finish through Ederson's legs, and then Harry set up the second for Giovani Lo Celso.

'Hurraaaaaaaay!' The Tottenham players celebrated together as one big happy, winning team. Mourinho's gameplan was working perfectly: stay strong in defence and then set Son Heung-min and Harry free on the counter-attack.

Even though other teams now knew what to expect, they still couldn't stop them. In the North London derby against Arsenal, Harry passed the ball to Son Heung-min as he crossed the halfway line. He still had a long way to go, but as he dribbled forward, the defenders backed away, so Son Heung-min decided to shoot from distance. Why not? His confidence was sky-high, and his accuracy was amazing! BANG!...

Gooooooooooooooooooooaaaaaaaaaaaaaaaaallllllllllllll llllllllllll!!!!!!!!!!!!!!!!!!!

What a wonderstrike! But these days, Son Heung-min was scoring so many goals that he didn't even bother with big celebrations. Instead, he just pointed up at the fans who were finally back in the Tottenham Hotspur Stadium, as if to say, 'That one was for you!'

And just before half-time, Tottenham's star strikers teamed up again. One second, Arsenal were on the attack, and the next, their North London rivals were breaking away with the ball. Serge gave it to Giovani, who played it forward to Son Heung-min. This time, he decided to pass, rather than shoot, and Harry happily smashed it in. *2–0!*

Yesssss, another classic Tottenham counterattack! As Son Heung-min celebrated with Harry, a huge smile spread across his face. He had ten goals and three assists already and they weren't even halfway through the season yet. After years of hard work, learning and progress, his childhood dream had finally come true. At last, it was official: Son Heung-min was now a Premier League superstar.

Turn the page for a sneak preview of
another brilliant football story by
Matt and Tom Oldfield. . .

FIRMINO

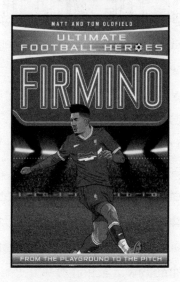

Available now!

CHAPTER 1

CLUB CHAMPIONS OF THE WORLD!

Club Champions of the World!

A loud cheer went up around the packed stadium as Jordan Henderson led the Liverpool team out on to the pitch for the 2019 FIFA Club World Cup Final. The 45,000 spectators couldn't wait to watch the European Champions in action.

Manager Jürgen Klopp had picked a strong team for the big match, full of entertaining superstars: the amazing goalkeeper, Alisson; the classy centre-back, Virgil van Dijk; and flying full-backs, Trent Alexander-Arnold and Andy Robertson. Most famous of all were the fab front three: Sadio Mané, Mo Salah and Roberto

Firmino. When they played together, Liverpool always scored, and they almost always won.

Although Sadio and Mo usually got more of the goals and the glory, everyone knew that Roberto Firmino was an equally important player. He connected with his teammates like the conductor in an orchestra. Without him, Liverpool simply weren't the same team. Firmino had the speed and skill to lead the counter-attacks, and the grit and determination to form the first line of their defence. Liverpool was very lucky to have him; there was no-one else quite like him in the world!

And Roberto had three major reasons to feel extra excited about the Club World Cup Final:

1) He had the chance to win a fourth top trophy of the year,

2) He had already scored the winner in the semi-final against Monterrey,

and 3) Liverpool were taking on the South American champions, Flamengo, who were from Brazil, just like him!

Roberto was lining up against several of his national teammates: Gabriel Barbosa, Filipe Luís, Diego Alves,

Rafinha… it was like a *Seleção* reunion! Although it was nice to see so many familiar faces, it also made him even more determined to win. After all, if Liverpool lost, he would never hear the end of it!

Plus, Roberto wanted to put on a show for all the people watching back in Brazil. He had recently helped his country to win the 2019 Copa América, but he hadn't played club football in his homeland since the age of eighteen. After his first senior season at Figueirense, he had joined German club Hoffenheim to try and make it big in Europe. And look at him now – he was a Champions League winner!

Back in Brazil, however, he still wasn't at that superstar level with Neymar Jr and his friend Philippe Coutinho. Not yet, anyway.

'This is my time to shine!' Firmino thought as he raced forward, right from the kick-off.

And his first scoring chance arrived straight away. Joe Gomez's long ball from the back flew all the way over the Flamengo defence and dropped down in front of Roberto inside the penalty area. Wow, what an opportunity to give Liverpool the lead! He chested the ball down beautifully, but when he saw the keeper rushing out towards him, he lost his cool and skied his shot high over the crossbar.

'Nooooo!' he groaned as he skidded across the grass on his knees.

It was a massive opportunity wasted, and Roberto regretted it more and more as the first half went on. Hopefully, he could make up for it in the second...

He ran into the Flamengo box, flicked the ball brilliantly over the defender's head and then fired off a left-foot shot. The keeper could only stand and watch as the ball flew straight past him... but bounced back off the post and then off the pitch for a goal kick.

What?! Roberto couldn't believe it, but he didn't stop for a strop. Instead, he kept going, hunting for his next chance.

At last, it arrived, in the first half of extra time. As Hendo played a long pass towards Sadio, Roberto was only just crossing the halfway line. But by the time Sadio controlled it and looked up for support, Roberto had sprinted forwards to the edge of the box to help him.

'Yes!'

Again, Roberto was one-on-one with the Flamengo keeper. This time, he didn't panic and blast the ball high and wide. Instead, he fooled everyone by calmly cutting inside. Then, with the keeper stranded on the floor, he fired a shot into the empty net to break millions of Brazilian hearts.

Goooooooooooooooooooooaaaaaaaaaaaaaaaalllllllllllllll llllllllllll!!!!!!!!!!!!!!!!!!!!!

Once he had seen the ball safely cross the line, Roberto ripped off his shirt and leapt high into the air, his trademark smile replaced by a look of pure passion. Yes, he had done it – he had made up for his earlier miss, and now Liverpool were minutes away from becoming the Club Champions of the World!

At the final whistle, there were hugs and high-fives all around. Job done – would Roberto ever get tired of that trophy-winning feeling? No, never! The biggest moments of the biggest games – that's when he was at his best. The boy from Maceió was a born matchwinner.

Tottenham

🏆 UEFA Champions League runner-up:
2018–19

South Korea

🏆 AFC Asian Cup runner-up: 2015
🏆 Asian Games U23: 2018

Individual

🏆 Korean Footballer of the Year: 2013, 2014,
2017, 2019, 2020
🏆 AFC Asian Cup Team of the Tournament: 2015

🏆 Asian International Footballer of the Year:
2015, 2017, 2019

🏆 Premier League Player of the Month:
September 2016, April 2017, October 2020

🏆 Tottenham Player of the Year: 2019, 2020

🏆 Premier League Goal of the Season: 2019–20

🏆 BBC Goal of the Season: 2019–20

🏆 FIFA Puskás Award for Best Goal of the Year: 2020

🏆 Asian Footballer of the Year: 2020

SON

7

THE FACTS

NAME:
Son Heung-min

DATE OF BIRTH:
8 July 1992

AGE: 28

PLACE OF BIRTH:
Chuncheon, Gangwon

NATIONALITY: South Korea

BEST FRIEND: Harry Kane

CURRENT CLUB: Tottenham

POSITION: LW/CF

THE STATS

Height (cm):	183
Club appearances:	428
Club goals:	151
Club trophies:	0
International appearances:	89
International goals:	26
International trophies:	1
Ballon d'Ors:	0

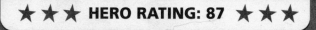

★ ★ ★ **HERO RATING: 87** ★ ★ ★

GREATEST MOMENTS

30 OCTOBER 2010,
FC KÖLN 3–2 HAMBURG

Son Heung-min's Bundesliga debut was delayed due
to injury, but when at last it arrived, he really made
the most of it. With his right foot, he flicked the ball
over the Köln keeper's head and then with his left
foot, coolly passed it into the empty net. At the age
of eighteen, he had just become Hamburg's youngest-
ever scorer and one of the Bundesliga's brightest
new talents.

9 NOVEMBER 2013,
BAYER LEVERKUSEN 5–3 HAMBURG

Soon after he became Bayer Leverkusen's new-record buy, Son Heung-min showed everyone that he was worth the money by scoring this brilliant hat-trick against his old club. The speed, the skill, the sensational shooting with both feet – yes, Son Heung-min was all set to become one of the most exciting attackers in Europe.

1 SEPTEMBER 2018,
SOUTH KOREA 2–1 JAPAN

After years of trying, the Asian Games represented Son Heung-min's last chance to win a trophy for South Korea before he turned twenty-eight, and therefore avoid two years of military service. As captain, he led his nation all the way to glory, setting up both of his team's extra-time goals in the final. Success, at last!

4 17 APRIL 2019, MANCHESTER CITY 4–3 TOTTENHAM

Although Spurs lost this incredible Champions League quarter-final second leg, they still progressed to the semi-finals on away goals. Son Heung-min played a very important part in his team's victory, scoring two at the Etihad, as well as the winner in the first leg at the new Tottenham Hotspur Stadium.

5 7 DECEMBER 2019, TOTTENHAM 5–0 BURNLEY

This was the day when Son became 'Sonaldo'. After collecting the ball on the edge of his own box, he raced forward on a seventy-yard sprint, dribbling all the way through the Burnley defence to score. Sonny's solo worldie went on to win the prize for Premier League Goal of the Season, and also the Puskás Award for the best goal in the whole world that year.

PLAY LIKE YOUR HEROES

THE SON HEUNG-MIN
SPRINT & SHOOT

STEP 1: Are you ready for hours and hours of hard, repetitive work? You'll need to keep taking shots with both feet until you can't even tell which one is stronger. Only then, will you be ready to progress to the next step...

STEP 2: Whether you're attacking or defending, always stay alert. Because as soon as your opponent makes a mistake, or your team's best passer gets the ball, it's time for you to...

STEP 3: *ZOOM!* Sprint towards goal as fast as you can, bursting in between the defenders and leaving them trailing far behind.

STEP 4: Once you've won the race to the ball, it's time to slow down and think smart. What do you need to do next in order to score?

STEP 5: If somehow there's still a defender in your way, use your strength and stepover skills to escape. But it's more likely that you're now one on one with the keeper, who is rushing out towards you...

STEP 6: *BANG!* Whether you're on your left foot or your right (remember, it doesn't matter anymore because they're as brilliant as each other!), stay calm and fire a low, hard and accurate shot into the bottom corner, just like you've practised thousands of times.

STEP 7: *GOAL!* As the ball hits the back of the net, race away smiling to celebrate with your teammates.

TEST YOUR KNOWLEDGE

QUESTIONS

1. What punishment did Son Woong-jung set for his sons if they weren't taking his training sessions seriously?

2. Which three top European nations did South Korea beat at the 2002 World Cup?

3. How old was Son Heung-min when he first went to Germany?

4. Which two former Premier League players helped Son Heung-min to improve at Hamburg?

5. Son Heung-min scored on his Bundesliga debut – True or False?

6. Which current Arsenal player did Son Heung-min play alongside at Bayer Leverkusen?

7. Mauricio Pochettino first tried to sign Son Heung-min when he was the manager of which club?

8. How much did Tottenham pay to sign Son Heung-min?

9. Which hero did Son Heung-min overtake to become the top scoring Asian player in Premier League history?

10. Who scored the first goal at the new Tottenham Hotspur Stadium when it opened in April 2019?

11. How many World Cup goals has Son Heung-min scored so far for South Korea?

Answers below. . . No cheating!

1. They had to do four hours of keepy-uppies without dropping the ball! 2. Portugal, Italy and Spain. 3. Sixteen. 4. Ruud van Nistelrooy and Rafael van der Vaart. 5. True, and he was only eighteen at the time! 6. Bernd Leno. 7. Southampton. 8. £22 million. 9. Park Ji-sung. 10. Son Heung-min, of course! 11. Three – one in 2014 and two in 2018.